I0820551

HOW TO LISTEN

ANCIENT WISDOM FOR MODERN READERS

■ ■ ■ ■

For a full list of titles in the series, go to https://press.princeton.edu/series/ancient-wisdom-for-modern-readers.

How to Listen: An Ancient Guide to Learning from Others
by Plutarch

How to Compete: An Ancient Guide to the Virtues of Sports
by Lucian

How to Find Happiness: An Ancient Guide to the Good Life
by Marcus Tullius Cicero

How to Be Grateful: An Aztec Guide to the Art of Gratitude
by Pablo of Texcoco

How to Cope: An Ancient Guide to Enduring Hardship
by Boethius

How to Feel: An Ancient Guide to Minding Our Emotions
by the Buddha

How to Be Caring: An Ancient Guide to a Compassionate Life
by Shantideva

How to Make a Home: An Ancient Guide to Style and Comfort
by Vitruvius and Guests

How to Have Willpower: An Ancient Guide to Not Giving In
by Plutarch and Prudentius

How to Talk about Love: An Ancient Guide for Modern Lovers
by Plato

How to Eat: An Ancient Guide for Healthy Living
by a Buffet of Ancient Authors

HOW TO LISTEN

■ ■ ■ ■ ■

An Ancient Guide to Learning from Others

Plutarch

Translated and introduced by Jeffrey Beneker

PRINCETON UNIVERSITY PRESS
PRINCETON & OXFORD

Published by Princeton University Press
41 William Street, Princeton, New Jersey 08540
99 Banbury Road, Oxford OX2 6JX

press.princeton.edu

GPSR Authorized Representative: Easy Access System Europe - Mustamäe tee 50, 10621 Tallinn, Estonia, gpsr.requests@easproject.com

ISBN 9780691265582
ISBN (e-book) 9780691265599

Library of Congress Control Number 2025946678

British Library Cataloging-in-Publication Data is available

Editorial: Rob Tempio and Chloe Coy
Production Editorial: Ali Parrington
Text and Jacket Design: Heather Hansen
Production: Erin Suydam
Publicity: William Pagdatoon and Charlotte Coyne

Jacket image: Filippo Tagliolini, *Attributed to Aristotle and Alexander*. Courtesy of Casa d'aste Capitolium Art.

This book has been composed in Stempel Garamond and Adobe Text Pro with Futura Std

Printed in the United States of America

1 3 5 7 9 10 8 6 4 2

In memoriam Philippi Stadter
magistri humanissimi

CONTENTS

Introduction ix

How to Listen 1

Notes 109

Further Reading 121

INTRODUCTION

> Listening well is the foundation for living well.
>
> —PLUTARCH OF CHAERONEA, *HOW TO LISTEN* 31

Who among us does *not* want to live well? All of us, I suspect, want a good life, but in considering the maxim quoted above, we might pause to ask what exactly "living well" entails. For Plutarch, living well meant living a philosophical life. Now, that sort of life might conjure the image of a person who has forsaken social interaction and mundane pursuits to withdraw into the solitary

contemplation of intriguing but largely academic problems. This, however, is really the opposite of what Plutarch had in mind. For him, living well according to philosophy meant living among family, friends, and fellow citizens, and it involved active engagement with all fields of knowledge and regular participation in learned discourse. He emphasized especially the study of ethics, with the aim of improving one's own character. Socrates famously claimed that "the unexamined life is not worth living."[1] Plutarch certainly agreed, though he would have been quick to stress Socrates's larger point, that self-examination makes life worth living because it leads to self-improvement. He endorsed, therefore, a practical system of ethics—as opposed to a merely theoretical one—that could become a guide to self-examination and self-

improvement through the development of good habits and, eventually, good character. This notion of practical ethics could be useful in all sorts of real-life contexts, ranging from the personal (controlling one's emotions and irrational impulses) to the social (becoming less talkative or inquisitive) to the political (cultivating a philanthropic approach to civic leadership). Defined in this way, "living well" is probably a goal that anyone reading a how-to book has already adopted and even recommitted to many times in their life, perhaps as recently as last New Year's Eve.

If living well is our destination, then according to Plutarch, listening well puts us on the right path. Listening allows us to acquire knowledge, to engage in dialogue, and above all to learn the system of ethics that will improve our life. It is so fundamental to the

formation of our character that even when we are children, our parents must monitor what we hear, to ensure that what is spoken to us is beneficial and not corrupting. Listening also plays a crucial role during our secondary and advanced education, in our adolescent and young-adult years when we hear the lessons that contribute most to the formation of our character and set the trajectory for the rest of our lives. And listening as adults allows us to continue to learn, to examine ourselves, and to form better habits.

Plutarch understood that as humans we are typically born with an innate ability to listen, but he also knew from his own experience that listening *well* does not come naturally. In *How to Listen*, he offers himself as a guide to developing and deploying this essential life skill. A native of Greece and citizen of Rome, Plutarch was a gifted scholar

and prolific author who also played an active role in local politics and was immersed in the intellectual world of the early Roman empire. He had close relationships with his family and a wide network of friends that extended from his local community in Chaeronea to the highest levels of the Roman governing class. His family and friends were the recipients of his philosophical essays and biographical writings, often addressed by name in the introductions, and they frequently appear as characters in his literary dialogues. In these writings, Plutarch comes across as sympathetic and humane, though he appears to have considered himself first and foremost a teacher. It is easy to form the impression that he could hardly allow a teachable moment to pass without a well-meaning intervention. His surviving works include several essays that

sought to provide guidance to friends and family as they experienced difficult or transitional moments in their lives. His essay *Advice to the Bride and Groom*, for example, is addressed to a newly married couple, Euridice and Pollianus, who were Plutarch's friends and former students. He urges them to think carefully—that is, philosophically—about their roles as spouses and provides them with a collection of examples drawn from history, myth, and literature that illustrate the sorts of good character and behavior that are, in Plutarch's view, critical to a successful marriage. When his young daughter died while he was away from home, he composed a consolation for his wife, Timoxena, which acknowledges her grief but also encourages her to respond with restraint and dignity. And he wrote an essay called *How to Study Poetry* for his

friend Marcus Sedatus, whose adolescent son was just beginning his secondary education, or as we might say, just entering high school. He advises Marcus about how to guide his son in the study of literature, which Plutarch views as preparation for the study of philosophy, the final and most important stage of a young person's educational journey.

That stage of the journey—the study of philosophy—is the subject of the "intervention" translated in this volume. *How to Listen* is addressed to Nicander, a young man who is the equivalent of today's first-year college student, having finished his study of literature and perhaps having studied rhetoric as well. Now a man, Nicander is recently independent of his father and his tutors, who previously guided his schooling (and directed his life in general), and so he

must take responsibility for himself. This has always been an exciting age, in both the ancient and the modern worlds: Young people are leaving home and deciding for themselves what to do, whom to associate with, and what to study, finding themselves free of supervision but perhaps not realizing how difficult it can be to make good decisions. Thus, Plutarch addresses his advice directly to Nicander rather than to his father, as he did when advising Marcus Sedatus about his high-school-age son. Plutarch warns his freshman advisee not to be led astray by his own impulses and desires, which, if left unchecked, can quickly take over the guiding role previously played by his father and lead him into all sorts of unhealthy behavior. He urges Nicander to adopt the view that independence does not mean a complete lack of supervision, but it

entails selecting the right guide. Reason, Plutarch argues, should become the guiding light of Nicander's advanced education. Only Reason can tame those internal, irrational impulses and desires, and so only Reason can ensure that the young man remains mindful of his studies.

Adopting Reason as one's guide is the cornerstone of listening well, but Plutarch understands that accepting any guidance at all may be unappealing to the young, newly independent Nicander. Thus, we see the importance of the study of literature—or pre-philosophy—in the earlier stage of education. Nicander might have had difficulty understanding or accepting Plutarch's line of argument without some prior exposure to ethics and, perhaps more important, some concrete examples of the consequences that follow both good and bad behavior.

(Reading about the disastrous consequences of Achilles's anger and rash actions in the *Iliad*, to take one example, might have shown him the danger of making snap decisions under the influence of strong emotions.) Plutarch, however, seems confident that Nicander, despite his lack of formal study and his youthful spirit, will accept his premise and realize, as he stands on the threshold of adulthood, that this is the moment to take stock of himself, to make conscious decisions about the person he wants to be, and to develop the habits that will allow him to become that person, not only while a student but for the rest of his life.

Plutarch assumes that Nicander possesses a high level of maturity and a real desire to learn from his advanced studies. This makes his advice valuable even for readers who are well beyond college age and who find them-

selves listening to learn in a variety of formal and informal situations. Drawing on his own experience learning from esteemed philosophers and teaching both youths and adults, Plutarch imagines a role for the student that is complex and demanding, and which leads to outcomes that are truly transformative. Effective listening entails much more than sitting quietly and absorbing lessons. It involves open-mindedness, critical thinking, deliberation, and the exercise of self-control, all habits that must first be learned through philosophy and then developed through practice. Higher education, therefore, becomes the training ground for people who wish to engage in a life-long pursuit of knowledge and self-improvement. "For the mind isn't like a container that needs filling," Plutarch explains. "It's like firewood that only needs a spark to ignite a

motivation for discovery and an appetite for the truth."[2] He encourages Nicander, therefore, to develop habits that will foster his intellectual curiosity and allow him to live an authentic, philosophical life.

The transformation that Plutarch imagines is no easy task. In his essay, he describes the challenges that Nicander will face, and which in fact confront all of us who wish to listen well. Plutarch does not so much offer solutions as point out the sorts of bad behavior that listeners should avoid and the good behavior they should emulate. The focus, then, is on the choices we make, and in this sense, Plutarch is acting as the reader's voice of Reason to help in the making of good choices. For example, a significant obstacle to effective listening is the fact that we are trained as students to demonstrate our intelligence by speaking up, while learn-

ing requires maintaining silence and thinking carefully about what is being said. Dialogue, Plutarch admits, certainly plays an important role in learning, but listeners must ask thoughtful questions and make meaningful contributions, and they must avoid the temptation to interrupt the speaker and turn the spotlight on themselves. Recognizing the importance of silence and suppressing the impulse to speak immediately is the first step in becoming a good listener. There are other issues as well. Good listeners must avoid being envious of a speaker who commands attention; they must offer constructive criticism of the speaker's argument and not simply tear it down; they must learn to appreciate the content of a lecture without being overly influenced by its style; they must prioritize the internal examination of themselves over the external criticism of

others; in formulating questions, they must focus on what is important and stay on topic; they must not attempt to dominate the dialogue that follows a lecture; and they must give themselves time to develop, since learning to listen well is a long process. These are the sorts of challenges that Plutarch brings to the reader's attention and the sorts of behavior that he recommends.

Plutarch knew that Nicander would be learning philosophy in a relatively unstructured environment, which made his intervention in the young man's education even more crucial. Ancient accounts of philosophers' classrooms reveal a high level of learned discourse but also hint that students could expect very little discipline. For example, the philosopher Plotinus, rather than teach from a written lesson plan, allowed his

students to set the syllabus by asking questions based on their own interests, and so his class meetings were known for their disorder and irrelevant conversations. When one of his students kept him talking for three days about a single subject, another student tried to intervene out of frustration, but Plotinus was uninterested in ensuring equal participation and allowed the first student to continue his questioning.[3] In *How to Listen*, Plutarch warns Nicander that he, too, will find himself in a chaotic learning environment, since he cannot assume that his fellow students will behave or that his instructor will keep them in line. Nicander's classmates are likely to be competitive and eager to demonstrate their knowledge, whether they understand the lessons or not; they may offer effusive praise after hearing even bad lectures, at times going so far as to give a standing ovation, just to

win their teacher's approval; and they will probably attempt to drown out Nicander when he speaks, or they may mock what he has to say. To succeed in an environment like that, a good student must find ways to maintain focus regardless of how poorly others are behaving.

Listening well, therefore, involves meeting challenges that come from both within and without. The practical ethics that Plutarch teaches in *How to Listen* prepare new students to take their first steps, while the more advanced lessons that they will learn in class allow them to continue making progress. Learning at all stages of life is a struggle, but Plutarch would argue that the struggle is essential and rewarding for anyone who wishes to live well.

▪▪▪

The Greek text published here comes from Plutarch, *Moralia*, volume 1 (Harvard University Press 1927) in the Loeb Classical Library, with only minor changes. I have divided the essay into more sections than the Loeb edition and renumbered the sections accordingly. This essay is also commonly known by the Latin titles *De recta ratione audiendi* and *De audiendo*.

ΠΕΡΙ ΤΟΥ ΑΚΟΥΕΙΝ

HOW TO LISTEN

[1] Τὴν γενομένην μοι σχολὴν περὶ τοῦ ἀκούειν, ὦ Νίκανδρε, ἀπέσταλκά σοι γράψας, ὅπως εἰδῇς τοῦ πείθοντος ὀρθῶς ἀκούειν, ὅτε τῶν προσταττόντων ἀπήλλαξαι τὸ ἀνδρεῖον ἀνειληφὼς ἱμάτιον. ἀναρχία μὲν γάρ, ἣν ἔνιοι τῶν νέων ἐλευθερίαν ἀπαιδευσίᾳ νομίζουσι, χαλεπωτέρους ἐκείνων τῶν ἐν παισὶ διδασκάλων καὶ παιδαγωγῶν δεσπότας ἐφίστησι τὰς ἐπιθυμίας ὥσπερ ἐκ δεσμῶν λυθείσας· καὶ καθάπερ Ἡρόδοτός φησιν ἅμα τῷ χιτῶνι συνεκδύεσθαι τὴν αἰδῶ τὰς γυναῖκας, οὕτως ἔνιοι τῶν νέων ἅμα τῷ τὸ παιδικὸν ἱμάτιον ἀποθέσθαι συναποθέμενοι τὸ αἰδεῖσθαι καὶ φοβεῖσθαι καὶ λύσαντες τὴν κατασχηματίζουσαν αὐτοὺς περιβολὴν εὐθὺς ἐμπίπλανται τῆς ἀναγωγίας. σὺ δὲ πολλάκις ἀκηκοὼς ὅτι ταὐτόν ἐστι τὸ ἕπεσθαι θεῷ καὶ τὸ πείθεσθαι λόγῳ, νόμιζε τὴν εἰς ἄνδρας ἐκ παίδων ἀγωγὴν οὐκ ἀρχῆς εἶναι τοῖς εὖ φρονοῦσιν ἀποβολήν, ἀλλὰ μεταβολὴν

[1] I've written up my old lecture on listening, my dear Nicander, and am sending it to you so that you'll know how to listen properly when someone is instructing you. The time is right, since you've come of age and are free of the guardians who used to supervise your learning.[1] But a lack of supervision, which some young people ignorantly believe to be freedom, releases from their chains, so to speak, those desires that become even more difficult masters than the teachers and tutors of one's youth. And just as Herodotus says that a woman sheds her dignity along with her dress,[2] likewise many young people, when they set aside their childhood clothing, also set aside reverence and respect, and once they've taken off the attire that marked their youth, they become completely undisciplined. You yourself have often heard it said that to follow God and

ἄρχοντος, ἀντὶ μισθωτοῦ τινος ἢ ἀργυρωνήτου θεῖον ἡγεμόνα τοῦ βίου λαμβάνουσι τὸν λόγον, ᾧ τοὺς ἑπομένους ἄξιόν ἐστι μόνους ἐλευθέρους νομίζειν. μόνοι γὰρ ἃ δεῖ βούλεσθαι μαθόντες, ὡς βούλονται ζῶσι· ταῖς δ᾽ ἀπαιδεύτοις καὶ παραλόγοις ὁρμαῖς καὶ πράξεσιν ἀγεννὲς ἔνεστί τι καὶ μικρὸν ἐν πολλῷ τῷ μετανοοῦντι τὸ ἑκούσιον.

[2] Ἐπεὶ δ᾽ ὥσπερ τῶν ἐγγραφομένων εἰς τὰς πολιτείας οἱ μὲν ἀλλοδαποὶ καὶ ξένοι κομιδῇ πολλὰ μέμφονται καὶ δυσκολαίνουσι τῶν γιγνομένων, οἱ δ᾽ ἐκ μετοίκων σύντροφοι καὶ συνήθεις τῶν νόμων ὄντες οὐ χαλεπῶς

to obey Reason are one and the same thing: Believe, therefore, that for those who think rightly, the transition from childhood to adulthood does not entail the rejection of supervision, but it means a change in supervisors. Those who adopt Reason as the divine guide for their life, in place of some hired tutor, are the only people worthy to be called free. For they alone, since they've learned what one ought to wish for, live as they wish. Conversely, there is nothing noble in acting on undisciplined and irrational impulses, and personal choice usually plays little role when a person repents of their actions.

[2] Consider the people who are enrolled as new citizens in a city: Those who come from abroad and are entirely foreign complain about and struggle with much of what occurs in their new home, while those who

προσδέχονται τὰ ἐπιβάλλοντα καὶ στέργουσιν, οὕτω σε δεῖ πολὺν χρόνον ἐν φιλοσοφίᾳ παρατρεφόμενον καὶ πᾶν μάθημα καὶ ἄκουσμα παιδικὸν ἀπ᾽ ἀρχῆς ἐθισθέντα προσφέρεσθαι λόγῳ φιλοσόφῳ μεμιγμένον, εὐμενῆ καὶ οἰκεῖον ἥκειν εἰς φιλοσοφίαν, ἣ μόνη τὸν ἀνδρεῖον καὶ τέλειον ὡς ἀληθῶς ἐκ λόγου τοῖς νέοις περιτίθησι κόσμον.

[3] Οὐκ ἂν ἀηδῶς δ᾽ οἶμαί σε προακοῦσαι περὶ τῆς ἀκουστικῆς αἰσθήσεως, ἣν ὁ Θεόφραστος παθητικωτάτην εἶναί φησι πασῶν. οὔτε γὰρ ὁρατὸν οὐδὲν οὔτε γευστὸν οὔθ᾽ ἁπτὸν ἐκστάσεις ἐπιφέρει καὶ ταραχὰς καὶ πτοίας τηλικαύτας ἡλίκαι καταλαμβάνουσι τὴν ψυχὴν κτύπων τινῶν καὶ πατάγων καὶ

were raised in the city as resident aliens and are accustomed to the local laws accept their lot quite easily and are content. And so it is with you, who for a long time have been exposed to philosophy in your upbringing and from the beginning have been accustomed to hearing all your lessons and childhood sayings expressed in philosophical language. You must approach philosophy with familiarity and an open mind, since philosophy alone bestows on young people the perfect, adult polish that is truly based on Reason.

[3] I think you'll be pleased to read an introductory discussion about the sense of hearing, which Theophrastus claims is the most impressionable of all the senses.[3] For nothing seen or tasted or touched delivers the same excitement or tumult or fright to the soul as when a person hears certain

ἤχων τῇ ἀκοῇ προσπεσόντων. ἔστι δὲ λογικωτέρα μᾶλλον ἢ παθητικωτέρα. τῇ μὲν γὰρ κακίᾳ πολλὰ χωρία καὶ μέρη τοῦ σώματος παρέχει δι᾽ αὐτῶν ἐνδῦσαν ἅψασθαι τῆς ψυχῆς, τῇ δ᾽ ἀρετῇ μία λαβὴ τὰ ὦτα τῶν νέων ἐστίν, ἂν καθαρὰ καὶ ἄθρυπτα κολακείᾳ καὶ λόγοις ἄθικτα φαύλοις ἀπ᾽ ἀρχῆς φυλάττηται. διὸ καὶ Ξενοκράτης τοῖς παισὶ μᾶλλον ἢ τοῖς ἀθληταῖς ἐκέλευε περιάπτειν ἀμφωτίδας, ὡς ἐκείνων μὲν τὰ ὦτα ταῖς πληγαῖς, τούτων δὲ τοῖς λόγοις τὰ ἤθη διαστρεφομένων, οὐκ ἀνηκοΐαν οὐδὲ κωφότητα προμνώμενος, ἀλλὰ τῶν λόγων τοὺς φαύλους φυλάττεσθαι παραινῶν, πρὶν ἑτέρους χρηστούς ὥσπερ φύλακας ἐντραφέντας ὑπὸ φιλοσοφίας τῷ ἤθει τὴν μάλιστα κινουμένην αὐτοῦ καὶ ἀναπειθομένην χώραν κατασχεῖν. καὶ Βίας ὁ παλαιὸς Ἀμάσιδι, κελευσθεὶς τὸ χρηστότατον ὁμοῦ καὶ φαυλότατον ἐκπέμψαι κρέας τοῦ ἱερείου, τὴν γλῶτταν ἐξελὼν ἀπέπεμψεν, ὡς

crashes, clangs, and voices. Now, the sense of hearing is more rational than emotional, for many parts of the body allow vice to slip through and lay hold of the soul, but for young people, virtue's only means of access is through the ears, provided that, from a child's earliest days, the ears are kept unpolluted, uncontaminated by flattery, and unsullied by corrupting words. That's why Xenocrates proposed that children rather than boxers should wear ear protection, reasoning that it was only a boxer's ears that were disfigured by punches, while a child's character was disfigured by words.[4] He wasn't proposing, of course, that children should stop listening or become deaf. Rather, he was advising that we should protect children from corrupting types of speech, until the beneficial type, nurtured by philosophy and embedded in their character,

καὶ βλάβας καὶ ὠφελείας τοῦ λέγειν ἔχοντος μεγίστας. οἵ τε πολλοὶ τὰ μικρὰ παιδία καταφιλοῦντες αὐτοί τε τῶν ὤτων ἅπτονται κἀκεῖνα τοῦτο ποιεῖν κελεύουσιν, αἰνιττόμενοι μετὰ παιδιᾶς ὅτι δεῖ φιλεῖν μάλιστα τοὺς διὰ τῶν ὤτων ὠφελοῦντας.

[4] Ἐπεὶ ὅτι γε πάσης ἀκροάσεως ἀπειργόμενος ὁ νέος καὶ λόγου μηδενὸς γευόμενος οὐ μόνον ἄκαρπος ὅλως καὶ ἀβλαστὴς διαμένει πρὸς ἀρετήν, ἀλλὰ καὶ

has taken command like a guardian over those aspects of character that are especially malleable and easily seduced. Bias long ago had a similar idea: When Amasis ordered him to send over both the best and the worst cut of meat from a sacrificed animal, he cut out the tongue and sent that alone, on the ground that speech produces both the greatest harm and the greatest benefit.[5] And many people, when they give affectionate kisses to small children, hold them by the ears, and they urge the children to grab their ears, too. Thus, they hint in a playful way that the children should have special affection for those who are good to them in a way that involves the ears.

[4] It's obvious that a young person who's been completely deprived of instruction and has heard no lessons not only remains entirely fruitless and barren with respect to

διαστρέφοιτ᾽ ἂν πρὸς κακίαν, ὥσπερ ἐκ χώρας ἀκινήτου καὶ ἀργῆς ἄγρια πολλὰ τῆς ψυχῆς ἀναδιδούς, δῆλόν ἐστι. τὰς γὰρ ἐφ᾽ ἡδονὴν ὁρμὰς καὶ πρὸς πόνον ὑποψίας (οὐ θυραίους οὐδ᾽ ὑπὸ λόγων ἐπεισάκτους, ἀλλ᾽ ὥσπερ αὐτόχθονας οὔσας μυρίων παθῶν καὶ νοσημάτων πηγάς) ἂν ἐᾷ τις ἀφέτους ᾗ πεφύκασι χωρεῖν καὶ μὴ λόγοις χρηστοῖς ἀφαιρῶν ἢ παρατρέπων καταρτύῃ τὴν φύσιν, οὐκ ἔστιν ὃ τῶν θηρίων οὐκ ἂν ἡμερώτερον ἀνθρώπου φανείη.

[5] Διὸ δὴ μεγάλην μὲν ὠφέλειαν οὐκ ἐλάττω δὲ κίνδυνον τοῖς νέοις τοῦ ἀκούειν ἔχοντος, οἶμαι καλῶς ἔχειν καὶ πρὸς αὑτὸν ἀεὶ καὶ πρὸς ἕτερον διαλέγεσθαι περὶ τοῦ ἀκούειν. ἐπεὶ καὶ τούτῳ κακῶς τοὺς πλείστους χρωμένους ὁρῶμεν, οἳ λέγειν ἀσκοῦσι πρὶν

virtue but might even be perverted into vice and so experience lots of wild growth in the soul, like a plot of land that's left unworked and fallow. Consider our human tendencies to seek pleasure and to avoid strenuous effort, which are not something imported or learned from others, but are homegrown, so to speak, and the source of countless misfortunes and diseases. If you allow these tendencies to progress naturally and range freely, and if you don't tend to yourself by weeding them out or redirecting them under the influence of good teaching, you'll become wilder than any feral beast.

[5] And so, since listening entails great benefit but no less danger for young people, I think it's important always to be in dialogue, both with oneself and with others, about listening. This is especially true because I see most people approaching the

ἀκούειν ἐθισθῆναι· καὶ λόγων μὲν οἴονται μάθησιν εἶναι καὶ μελέτην, ἀκροάσει δὲ καὶ τοὺς ὁπωσοῦν χρωμένους ὠφελεῖσθαι. καίτοι τοῖς μὲν σφαιρίζουσιν ἅμα τοῦ βαλεῖν καὶ τοῦ λαβεῖν τὴν σφαῖραν ἡ μάθησις· ἐν δὲ τῇ τοῦ λόγου χρείᾳ τὸ δέξασθαι καλῶς τοῦ προέσθαι πρότερόν ἐστιν, ὥσπερ τοῦ τεκεῖν τὸ συλλαβεῖν καὶ κατασχεῖν τι τῶν γονίμων.

[6] Ταῖς μὲν οὖν ὄρνισι τὰς ὑπηνεμίους λοχείας καὶ ὠδῖνας ἀτελῶν τινων καὶ ἀψύχων ὑπολειμμάτων ὀχείας λέγουσιν εἶναι· τῶν δ᾽ ἀκούειν μὴ δυναμένων νέων μηδ᾽ ὠφελεῖσθαι δι᾽ ἀκοῆς ἐθισθέντων ὑπηνέμιος ὄντως ὁ λόγος ἐκπίπτων "ἀκλειὴς ἀίδηλος ὑπαὶ νεφέεσσι κεδάσθη." τὰ μὲν γὰρ ἀγγεῖα πρὸς τὴν ὑποδοχὴν τῶν ἐγχεομένων ἐπικλίνουσι καὶ συνεπιστρέφουσιν, ἵν᾽ ἔγχυσις ἀληθῶς, μὴ ἔκχυσις γένηται, αὐτοὺς δὲ τῷ λέγοντι

matter incorrectly: They practice speaking before they have been trained to listen. They believe that the art of speaking requires serious study but think they can listen however they like and still derive benefit. But learning to play ball means learning to catch as well as to throw, and so when it comes to dialogue, listening properly must come before speaking, just as conceiving and being pregnant must precede giving birth.

[6] They say that "wind eggs" produced by birds come from the incomplete and lifeless remnants of fertilization.[6] When young people are unable to listen or are not accustomed to deriving benefit from listening, the "wind words" that they produce are truly "unrenowned and unknown, and scattered across the sky."[7] For they will carefully tilt and turn their jugs under running water so that the liquid enters cleanly rather than

παρέχειν καὶ συναρμόττειν τῇ προσοχῇ τὴν ἀκρόασιν, ὡς μηδὲν ἐκφύγῃ τῶν χρησίμως λεγομένων, οὐ μανθάνουσιν, ἀλλ᾽ ὃ πάντων καταγελαστότατόν ἐστιν, ἂν μέν τινι προστύχωσι διηγουμένῳ δεῖπνον ἢ πομπὴν ἢ ὄνειρον ἢ λοιδορίαν γεγενημένην αὐτῷ πρὸς ἄλλον, ἀκροῶνται σιωπῇ καὶ προσλιπαροῦσιν· ἂν δέ τις αὐτοὺς ἐπισπασάμενος διδάσκῃ τι τῶν χρησίμων ἢ παραινῇ τῶν δεόντων ἢ νουθετῇ πλημμελοῦντας ἢ καταπραΰνῃ χαλεπαίνοντας, οὐχ ὑπομένουσιν, ἀλλ᾽ ἂν μὲν δύνωνται, περιγενέσθαι φιλοτιμούμενοι διαμάχονται πρὸς τὸν λόγον· εἰ δὲ μή, φεύγοντες ἀπίασι πρὸς ἑτέρους λόγους καὶ φλυάρους, ὡς ἀγγεῖα φαῦλα καὶ σαθρὰ τὰ ὦτα πάντων μᾶλλον ἢ τῶν ἀναγκαίων ἐμπιπλάντες. τοὺς μὲν οὖν ἵππους οἱ καλῶς τρέφοντες εὐστόμους τῷ χαλινῷ, τοὺς δὲ παῖδας εὐηκόους τῷ λόγῳ παρέχουσι, πολλὰ μὲν ἀκούειν μὴ πολλὰ δὲ λέγειν διδασκομένους. καὶ γὰρ τὸν

splashing out, but they never learn to open themselves to a person who's speaking or to listen attentively so that they don't miss any useful information. Rather—and this is the most ridiculous thing of all—when they run into someone who begins to tell them about a dinner or a parade or a dream or how they chewed someone out, they listen in silence and want to hear the whole story, but when someone pulls them aside to teach them something useful or give them necessary advice or caution them when they're making a mistake or calm them when they're upset, they won't put up with it. Instead, they fight back against what's being said and do their best to win the argument. And if they can't win, they run off in search of more frivolous stories, treating their ears as though they were cheap and cracked jars by filling them with everything except what's essential.

Ἐπαμεινώνδαν ὁ Σπίνθαρος ἐπαινῶν ἔφη μήτε πλείονα γιγνώσκοντι μήτ᾽ ἐλάττονα φθεγγομένῳ ῥᾳδίως ἐντυχεῖν ἑτέρῳ. καὶ τὴν φύσιν ἡμῶν ἑκάστῳ λέγουσι δύο μὲν ὦτα δοῦναι, μίαν δὲ γλῶτταν, ὡς ἐλάττονα λέγειν ἢ ἀκούειν ὀφείλοντι.

[7] Πανταχοῦ μὲν οὖν τῷ νέῳ κόσμος ἀσφαλής ἐστιν ἡ σιωπή, μάλιστα δ᾽ ὅταν ἀκούων ἑτέρου μὴ συνταράττηται μηδ᾽ ἐξυλακτῇ πρὸς ἕκαστον, ἀλλὰ κἂν ὁ λόγος ᾖ μὴ λίαν ἀρεστός, ἀνέχηται καὶ περιμένῃ παύσασθαι τὸν διαλεγόμενον, καὶ παυσαμένου μὴ εὐθέως ἐπιβάλλῃ τὴν ἀντίρρησιν, ἀλλ᾽ ὡς

Now, those who raise horses properly make them willing to accept the bit, while those who raise children properly make them willing to obey Reason. Properly raised children have been taught to listen much and speak little. Consider this example: When Spintharus was praising Epaminondas, he declared that it would be no easy task to find someone who knew more than Epaminondas but spoke less.[8] Here's another one: They say that nature gave each of us two ears but only one tongue, since we ought to listen more than we speak.

[7] In every situation, young people demonstrate their best behavior when they hold their tongue. This is especially true when they're listening to someone without getting agitated or growling at every point that's made, and even if the lecture isn't particularly pleasing, they're putting up with it

Αἰσχίνης φησί, διαλείπῃ χρόνον, εἴτε προσθεῖναί τι βούλοιτο τοῖς λελεγμένοις ὁ εἰρηκώς, εἴτε μεταθέσθαι καὶ ἀφελεῖν. οἱ δ᾽ εὐθὺς ἀντικόπτοντες, οὔτ᾽ ἀκούοντες οὔτ᾽ ἀκουόμενοι λέγοντες δὲ πρὸς λέγοντας, ἀσχημονοῦσιν· ὁ δ᾽ ἐγκρατῶς καὶ μετ᾽ αἰδοῦς ἀκούειν ἐθισθεὶς τὸν μὲν ὠφέλιμον λόγον ἐδέξατο καὶ κατέσχε, τὸν δ᾽ ἄχρηστον ἢ ψευδῆ μᾶλλον διεῖδε καὶ κατεφώρασε, φιλαλήθης φανείς, οὐ φιλόνεικος οὐδὲ προπετὴς καὶ δύσερις. ὅθεν οὐ κακῶς ἔνιοι λέγουσιν ὅτι δεῖ τῶν νέων μᾶλλον ἐκπνευματοῦν τὸ οἴημα καὶ τὸν τῦφον ἢ τῶν ἀσκῶν τὸν ἀέρα τοὺς ἐγχέαι τι βουλομένους χρήσιμον· εἰ δὲ μή, γέμοντες ὄγκου καὶ φυσήματος οὐ προσδέχονται.

and waiting for the speaker to pause. And when the pause comes, they don't immediately launch a counterattack, but as Aeschines says, they wait a moment, in case the speaker wishes to add something to what's been said, or to revise, or to take something back.[9] Students who are quick to cut people off, without listening or being heard themselves and speaking on top of others, only disgrace themselves. But students who are self-controlled and accustomed to listening respectfully hear and retain what's beneficial, while conversely, they see right through what's useless and false. They come across as seekers of the truth rather than as contentious, nor do they appear reckless or quarrelsome. For that reason, some rightly say that it's more important to rid young people of their self-importance and delusion than to deflate

[8] Φθόνος τοίνυν μετὰ βασκανίας καὶ δυσμενείας οὐδενὶ μὲν ἔργῳ παρὼν ἀγαθόν, ἀλλὰ πᾶσιν ἐμπόδιος τοῖς καλοῖς, κάκιστος δ᾽ ἀκροωμένῳ πάρεδρος καὶ σύμβουλος, ἀνιαρὰ καὶ ἀηδῆ καὶ δυσπρόσδεκτα ποιῶν τὰ ὠφέλιμα διὰ τὸ πᾶσι μᾶλλον ἥδεσθαι τοὺς φθονοῦντας ἢ τοῖς εὖ λεγομένοις. καίτοι πλοῦτος μὲν ὅντινα δάκνει καὶ δόξα καὶ κάλλος, ἑτέροις ὑπάρχοντα, φθονερός ἐστι μόνον· ἄχθεται γὰρ ἄλλων εὐτυχούντων· ὁ δὲ λόγῳ καλῶς λεγομένῳ δυσχεραίνων ὑπὸ τῶν ἰδίων ἀγαθῶν ἀνιᾶται. ὡς γὰρ τὸ φῶς τῶν βλεπόντων, καὶ ὁ λόγος τῶν ἀκουόντων ἀγαθόν ἐστιν, ἂν βούλωνται δέχεσθαι.

wineskins, if we wish to fill them with something useful. If we don't empty them first, the young will remain full of pretension and conceit, and thus they'll have no room for anything else.

[8] Envy, moreover, with its jealousy and ill will, is never an asset. Rather, it's an impediment to all good works, and it's the worst companion and advisor for someone who's trying to listen. It makes everything that's beneficial appear annoying, distasteful, and hard to swallow, since the person who's experiencing envy takes absolutely no pleasure in listening to someone who's speaking well. People who are pained by the wealth, reputation, or beauty that others possess are merely jealous, since they're annoyed at another's good fortune, but people who are disturbed by a well-delivered lecture are vexed by something that's actually

[9] Τὸν μὲν οὖν ἐφ᾽ ἑτέροις φθόνον ἄλλαι τινὲς ἀπαίδευτοι καὶ κακαὶ διαθέσεις ἐμποιοῦσιν, ὁ δὲ πρὸς τοὺς λέγοντας ἐκ φιλοδοξίας ἀκαίρου καὶ φιλοτιμίας ἀδίκου γεννώμενος οὐδὲ προσέχειν ἐᾷ τοῖς λεγομένοις τὸν οὕτω διακείμενον, ἀλλὰ θορυβεῖ καὶ περισπᾷ τὴν διάνοιαν, ἅμα μὲν τὴν ἑαυτῆς ἕξιν ἐπισκοποῦσαν εἰ λείπεται τῆς τοῦ λέγοντος, ἅμα δὲ τοὺς ἄλλους ἐπιβλέπουσαν εἰ ἄγανται καὶ θαυμάζουσιν, ἐκπληττομένην τε ὑπὸ τῶν ἐπαίνων καὶ ἀγριαίνουσαν πρὸς τοὺς παρόντας ἂν ἀποδέχωνται τὸν λέγοντα, τῶν δὲ λόγων τοὺς μὲν εἰρημένους ἐῶσαν καὶ προϊεμένην, ὅτι λυποῦσι μνημονευόμενοι, πρὸς δὲ τοὺς

good for them. For just as the light is good for people who are seeing, so the well-delivered lecture is good for those who are listening, provided they are receptive to its message.

[9] In most situations, envy arises from an ignorant and ignoble disposition, but the envy that's directed at people who are speaking is engendered by an untimely arrogance and an unjust love of honor, and it prevents the envious person from paying attention to what's being said. This sort of envy disrupts and distracts the mind, which at one moment is busy evaluating its own skills, to see if they fall short of the speaker's talents, and in the next moment is busy observing the other listeners, to see if they're amazed and impressed. The distracted mind is astonished when audience members offer praise and furious when they show approval;

λείποντας ταραττομένην καὶ τρέμουσαν μὴ τῶν εἰρημένων βελτίονες γένωνται, σπεύδουσαν δὲ τάχιστα παύσασθαι τοὺς λέγοντας ὅταν κάλλιστα λέγωσι, λυθείσης δὲ τῆς ἀκροάσεως πρὸς οὐδενὶ τῶν εἰρημένων οὖσαν ἀλλὰ τὰς φωνὰς καὶ διαθέσεις τῶν παρόντων ἐπιψηφίζουσαν, καὶ τοὺς μὲν ἐπαινοῦντας ὥσπερ ἐμμανῆ φεύγουσαν καὶ ἀποπηδῶσαν, προστρέχουσαν δὲ καὶ συναγελαζομένην τοῖς ψέγουσι τὰ εἰρημένα καὶ διαστρέφουσιν· ἂν δὲ μηδὲν ᾖ διαστρέψαι, παραβάλλουσαν ἑτέρους τινὰς ὡς ἄμεινον εἰρηκότας εἰς ταὐτὸ καὶ δυνατώτερον, ἕως διαφθείρασα καὶ λυμηναμένη τὴν ἀκρόασιν ἀχρεῖον ἑαυτῇ καὶ ἀνόνητον ἀπεργάσηται.

it willingly forgets what's already been said, since to recall the words only causes grief, and it worries about what's coming next, in case the lecture actually improves; it's eager for the speaker to finish quickly when they're speaking especially well, but when the lecture is finished, it disregards the contents and instead assesses the audience's response; it's almost manically repelled by those who offer praise, but it's immediately attracted to those who criticize what's been said and distort the message; and if there's nothing to distort, it compares the speaker to others who—supposedly—have spoken better and more powerfully on the same subject. In the end, the mind that's distracted by envy corrupts and abuses the listening experience so that it becomes entirely useless and unprofitable.

[10] Διὸ δεῖ τῇ φιληκοΐᾳ πρὸς τὴν φιλοδοξίαν σπεισάμενον ἀκροᾶσθαι τοῦ λέγοντος ἵλεων καὶ πρᾶον, ὥσπερ ἐφ᾽ ἑστίασιν ἱερὰν καὶ θυσίας ἀπαρχὴν παρειλημμένον, ἐπαινοῦντα μὲν ἐν οἷς ἐπιτυγχάνει τὴν δύναμιν, ἀγαπῶντα δὲ τὴν προθυμίαν αὐτὴν τοῦ φέροντος εἰς μέσον ἃ γιγνώσκει καὶ πείθοντος ἑτέρους δι᾽ ὧν αὐτὸς πέπεισται. τοῖς μὲν οὖν κατορθουμένοις ἐπιλογιστέον ὡς οὐκ ἀπὸ τύχης οὐδ᾽ αὐτομάτως ἀλλ᾽ ἐπιμελείᾳ καὶ πόνῳ καὶ μαθήσει κατορθοῦνται, καὶ μιμητέον γε ταῦτα θαυμάζοντάς γε δὴ καὶ ζηλοῦντας· τοῖς δ᾽ ἁμαρτανομένοις ἐφιστάναι χρὴ τὴν διάνοιαν, ὑφ᾽ ὧν αἰτιῶν καὶ ὅθεν ἡ παρατροπὴ γέγονεν. ὡς γὰρ ὁ Ξενοφῶν φησι τοὺς οἰκονομικοὺς καὶ ἀπὸ τῶν φίλων ὀνίνασθαι καὶ ἀπὸ τῶν ἐχθρῶν, οὕτω τοὺς ἐγρηγορότας καὶ προσέχοντας οὐ μόνον κατορθοῦντες ἀλλὰ καὶ διαμαρτάνοντες ὠφελοῦσιν οἱ λέγοντες·

[10] We must, therefore, make a truce between the love of listening and the love of glory, so we can attend a lecture with grace and mildness, as we would attend a holy banquet held after a sacrifice. We must praise the speaker's ability when the arguments are convincing, and when they're not, we must nonetheless appreciate the good intentions of someone who's shared their knowledge and attempted to teach us what they've learned. When a speaker does well, we must not assume that it was by luck or accident, but thanks to study and toil and learning, and we should admire and emulate their technique. And when a speaker doesn't do well, we should analyze their thought processes, to understand how and where their arguments went awry. For Xenophon says about the managers of estates that they benefit from both their friends and their

καὶ γὰρ διανοήματος εὐτέλεια καὶ ῥήματος κενότης καὶ σχῆμα φορτικὸν καὶ πτόησις μετὰ χαρᾶς ἀπειροκάλου πρὸς ἔπαινον καὶ ὅσα τοιαῦτα μᾶλλον ἀκροωμένοις ἐφ᾽ ἑτέρων ἢ λέγουσιν ἐφ᾽ ἑαυτῶν καταφαίνεται. διὸ δεῖ μεταφέρειν τὴν εὔθυναν ἐφ᾽ ἑαυτοὺς ἀπὸ τοῦ λέγοντος, ἀνασκοποῦντας εἴ τι τοιοῦτο λανθάνομεν ἁμαρτάνοντες. ῥᾷστον γάρ ἐστι τῶν ὄντων τὸ μέμψασθαι τὸν πλησίον, ἀχρήστως τε καὶ κενῶς γιγνόμενον, ἂν μὴ πρός τινα διόρθωσιν ἢ φυλακὴν ἀναφέρηται τῶν ὁμοίων. καὶ τὸ τοῦ Πλάτωνος οὐκ ὀκνητέον ἀεὶ πρὸς αὑτὸν ἐπὶ τῶν ἁμαρτανόντων ἀναφθέγγεσθαι, "μή που ἄρ᾽ ἐγὼ τοιοῦτος;" ὡς γὰρ ἐν τοῖς ὄμμασι τῶν πλησίον ἐλλάμποντα τὰ ἑαυτῶν ὁρῶμεν, οὕτως ἐπὶ τῶν λόγων δεῖ τοὺς ἑαυτῶν ἐνεικονίζεσθαι τοῖς ἑτέρων, ἵνα μήτ᾽ ἄγαν θρασέως καταφρονῶμεν ἄλλων, αὐτοῖς τε προσέχωμεν ἐν τῷ λέγειν ἐπιμελέστερον.

enemies.[10] So also with students who are vigilant and attentive: They derive a benefit from listening both when lectures are well delivered and when they're not. Certainly, weakness of thought, feebleness of expression, a vulgar figure of speech, emotion that's inelegantly expressed and meant to elicit praise—and other similar mistakes—are all better discovered when listening to someone else than when speaking yourself. That's why we must transfer our scrutiny away from the speaker and onto ourselves, to discern whether we're unconsciously making similar mistakes. For there is nothing in the world easier than finding fault with one's neighbor, but it's also a useless and pointless exercise, unless we convert our faultfinding into self-correction and avoid making the same errors. We should never hesitate to repeat to ourselves the

[11] Χρήσιμον δὲ πρὸς τοῦτο καὶ τὸ τῆς παραβολῆς, ὅταν γενόμενοι καθ᾽ αὑτοὺς ἀπὸ τῆς ἀκροάσεως καὶ λαβόντες τι τῶν μὴ καλῶς ἢ μὴ ἱκανῶς εἰρῆσθαι δοκούντων ἐπιχειρῶμεν εἰς ταὐτὸ καὶ προάγωμεν αὑτοὺς τὰ μὲν ὥσπερ ἀναπληροῦν, τὰ δ᾽ ἐπανορθοῦσθαι, τὰ δ᾽ ἑτέρως φράζειν, τὰ δ᾽ ὅλως ἐξ ὑπαρχῆς εἰσφέρειν πειρώμενοι πρὸς τὴν ὑπόθεσιν. ὃ καὶ Πλάτων ἐποίησε πρὸς τὸν Λυσίου λόγον. τὸ μὲν γὰρ ἀντειπεῖν οὐ χαλεπὸν ἀλλὰ καὶ

saying of Plato when we observe someone else making a mistake: "Am I perhaps doing the same thing?"[11] For just as we can see our own eyes reflected in the eyes of someone else, so we must look for a reflection of our own approach to speaking in the lectures of others.[12] That way, we won't be so quick to condemn others, and we'll be more attentive to ourselves, so that we speak more carefully.

[11] Comparative composition is also helpful in this process. It works like this: When a lecture's over and we're on our own, we select a topic that struck us as poorly or inadequately expressed and then tackle it ourselves. We elaborate some parts and revise others, we express some things differently, and we may even approach the topic from an entirely different angle. This, for example, is what Plato did for the speech

πάνυ ῥᾴδιον εἰρημένῳ λόγῳ· τὸ δ᾽ ἕτερον ἀνταναστῆσαι βελτίονα παντάπασιν ἐργῶδες. ὥσπερ ὁ Λακεδαιμόνιος ἀκούσας ὅτι Φίλιππος Ὄλυνθον κατέσκαψεν "ἀλλ᾽ οὐκ ἀναστῆσαί γε τοιαύτην" ἔφη "πόλιν ἐκεῖνος ἂν δυνηθείη." ὅταν οὖν ἐν τῷ διαλέγεσθαι πρὸς τὴν τοιαύτην ὑπόθεσιν μὴ πολὺ φαινώμεθα τῶν εἰρηκότων διαφέροντες, πολὺ τοῦ καταφρονεῖν ἀφαιροῦμεν, καὶ τάχιστα κολούεται τὸ αὔθαδες ἡμῶν καὶ φίλαυτον ἐν ταῖς τοιαύταις ἐλεγχόμενον ἀντιπαραβολαῖς.

[12] Τῷ τοίνυν καταφρονεῖν τὸ θαυμάζειν ἀντικείμενον εὐγνωμονεστέρας μέν ἐστι δήπου καὶ ἡμερωτέρας φύσεως, δεῖταί γε μὴν οὐδ᾽ αὐτὸ μικρᾶς εὐλαβείας, τάχα δὲ καὶ μείζονος· οἱ μὲν γὰρ καταφρονητικοὶ καὶ θρασεῖς ἧττον ὠφελοῦνται ὑπὸ τῶν λεγόντων,

of Lysias.[13] It's not hard—in fact, it's quite easy—to take issue with a spoken lecture. However, to replace a lecture with a new, better one requires great effort. As the Spartan man said when he heard that Philip had demolished the city of Olynthus: "Fine, but he could never rebuild it to be as good as it was!"[14] Therefore, whenever we're involved in dialogue about a particular topic and don't appear to be saying anything very different from what's been said before, we feel much less contempt for others, and our pride and arrogance are curtailed, as we're tested in this sort of comparative environment.

[12] Admiration, which is the opposite of contempt, arises, of course, from a more kindly and mild nature, but it requires a great deal of discretion, perhaps even more discretion than contempt. For even though contemptuous and impulsive people benefit

οἱ δὲ θαυμαστικοὶ καὶ ἄκακοι μᾶλλον βλάπτονται, καὶ τὸν Ἡράκλειτον οὐκ ἐλέγχουσιν εἰπόντα "βλὰξ ἄνθρωπος ἐπὶ παντὶ λόγῳ ἐπτοῆσθαι φιλεῖ." δεῖ δὲ τὸν μὲν ἔπαινον ἀφελῶς τοῖς λέγουσι τὴν δὲ πίστιν εὐλαβῶς προΐεσθαι τοῖς λόγοις, καὶ τῆς μὲν λέξεως καὶ προφορᾶς τῶν ἀγωνιζομένων εὐμενῆ καὶ ἁπλοῦν εἶναι θεατήν, τῆς δὲ χρείας καὶ τῆς ἀληθείας τῶν λεγομένων ἀκριβῆ καὶ πικρὸν ἐξεταστήν, ἵν᾽ οἱ μὲν λέγοντες μὴ μισῶσιν, οἱ δὲ λόγοι μὴ βλάπτωσιν· ὡς πολλὰ ψευδῆ καὶ πονηρὰ δόγματα λανθάνομεν εὐνοίᾳ καὶ πίστει τῇ πρὸς τοὺς λέγοντας ἐνδεχόμενοι. οἱ μὲν οὖν Λακεδαιμονίων ἄρχοντες ἀνδρὸς οὐκ εὖ βεβιωκότος γνώμην δοκιμάσαντες ἑτέρῳ προσέταξαν εἰπεῖν εὐδοκιμοῦντι περὶ τὸν βίον καὶ τὸ ἦθος, ὀρθῶς πάνυ καὶ πολιτικῶς ἐθίζοντες τὸν δῆμον ὑπὸ τοῦ τρόπου μᾶλλον ἢ τοῦ λόγου τῶν συμβουλευόντων ἄγεσθαι.

less from lectures, those who easily and naively express admiration suffer more harm, proving that Heraclitus was right when he said, "Fools tend to get excited about whatever they hear."[15] We must, then, be quick to bestow praise on a speaker, but use discretion when giving credence to a speech; we must be a friendly and sincere audience for a speaker's words and expressions, but scrupulous and exacting examiners of the utility and truth of what's being said, so that no speaker will hate us and no lecture will cause us harm. For without being aware of it, we accept many false and malicious doctrines by showing goodwill and trust to our instructors. Once, the magistrates of Sparta were in favor of a proposal suggested by a man they judged not to have lived an upright life, and so they ordered another man—one who had earned a good reputation for his

[13] Τοὺς δ᾽ ἐν φιλοσοφίᾳ λόγους ἀφαιροῦντα χρὴ τὴν τοῦ λέγοντος δόξαν αὐτοὺς ἐφ᾽ ἑαυτῶν ἐξετάζειν. ὡς γὰρ πολέμου, καὶ ἀκροάσεως πολλὰ τὰ κενά ἐστι. καὶ γὰρ πολιὰ τοῦ λέγοντος καὶ πλάσμα καὶ ὀφρῦς καὶ περιαυτολογία, μάλιστα δ᾽ αἱ κραυγαὶ καὶ οἱ θόρυβοι καὶ τὰ πηδήματα τῶν παρόντων συνεκπλήττει τὸν ἄπειρον ἀκροατὴν καὶ νέον ὥσπερ ὑπὸ ῥεύματος παραφερόμενον. ἔχει δέ τι καὶ ἡ λέξις ἀπατηλόν, ὅταν ἡδεῖα καὶ πολλὴ καὶ μετ᾽ ὄγκου τινὸς καὶ κατασκευῆς ἐπιφέρηται τοῖς πράγμασιν. ὡς γὰρ τῶν ὑπ᾽ αὐλοῖς ᾀδόντων αἱ πολλαὶ τοὺς ἀκούοντας ἁμαρτίαι διαφεύγουσιν, οὕτω περιττὴ καὶ σοβαρὰ λέξις

life and character—to present the proposal to the assembly: This was very much the right and civic-minded thing to do, since it trained the people to be guided more by the habits than by the speech of their advisors.

[13] But when it comes to philosophical instruction, we must disregard the speaker's reputation and examine the content of the lecture on its own terms, for in listening—as in war—we encounter a good deal of bluster and pretension. A speaker's graying hair, affectation, serious expression, and braggadocio, not to mention the ruckus of the audience as it shouts and springs to its feet—all these things startle the young and inexperienced listener, who's carried away as though on the current of a river. There's something deceptive in speech whenever it's pleasant and profuse, and when it addresses subjects with a certain majesty and

ἀντιλάμπει τῷ ἀκροατῇ πρὸς τὸ δηλούμενον. ὁ μὲν γὰρ Μελάνθιος, ὡς ἔοικε, περὶ τῆς Διογένους τραγῳδίας ἐρωτηθεὶς οὐκ ἔφη κατιδεῖν αὐτὴν ὑπὸ τῶν ὀνομάτων ἐπιπροσθουμένην· αἱ δὲ τῶν πολλῶν διαλέξεις καὶ μελέται σοφιστῶν οὐ μόνον τοῖς ὀνόμασι παραπετάσμασι χρῶνται τῶν διανοημάτων, ἀλλὰ καὶ τὴν φωνὴν ἐμμελείαις τισὶ καὶ μαλακότησι καὶ παρισώσεσιν ἐφηδύνοντες ἐκβακχεύουσι καὶ παραφέρουσι τοὺς ἀκροωμένους, κενὴν ἡδονὴν διδόντες καὶ κενοτέραν δόξαν ἀντιλαμβάνοντες. ὥστ᾽ αὐτοῖς συμβαίνει τὸ ὑπὸ Διονυσίου ῥηθέν. ἐκεῖνος γάρ, ὡς ἔοικεν, εὐδοκιμοῦντι κιθαρῳδῷ παρὰ τὴν θέαν ἐπαγγειλάμενος δωρεάς τινας μεγάλας ὕστερον οὐδὲν ἔδωκεν ὡς ἀποδεδωκὼς τὴν χάριν· "ὅσον γάρ," ἔφη, "χρόνον εὔφραινες ᾄδων, τοσοῦτον ἔχαιρες ἐλπίζων." τοῦτον δὲ τὸν ἔρανον αἱ τοιαῦται πληροῦσιν ἀκροάσεις τοῖς λέγουσι·

artistry. For just as most mistakes that singers make while accompanied by the aulos escape the audience, so an extravagant and rousing style of speaking can dazzle listeners so that they don't perceive the subject clearly.[16] That's apparently why Melanthius, when he was asked about Diogenes's play, said that it was obscured by all the words and so he didn't see it.[17] The discourses and lectures of most professors not only employ language in a way that camouflages their meaning, but by sweetening the delivery with gracefulness, delicacy, and balance, they also excite and seduce their listeners, producing in return empty pleasures and even emptier reputations for themselves. The audience thus experiences the witticism of Dionysius, who, while attending a concert, seems to have promised that he would give a great reward to a famous kithara

θαυμάζονται γὰρ ἐφ᾽ ὅσον τέρπουσιν, εἶθ᾽ ἅμα τῆς ἀκοῆς ἐξερρύη τὸ ἡδὺ κἀκείνους προλέλοιπεν ἡ δόξα, καὶ μάτην τοῖς μὲν ὁ χρόνος τοῖς δὲ καὶ ὁ βίος ἀνάλωται.

[14] Διὸ δεῖ τὸ πολὺ καὶ κενὸν ἀφαιροῦντα τῆς λέξεως αὐτὸν διώκειν τὸν καρπὸν καὶ μιμεῖσθαι μὴ τὰς στεφανηπλόκους ἀλλὰ τὰς μελίττας. αἱ μὲν γὰρ ἐπιλέγουσαι τὰ ἀνθηρὰ καὶ εὐώδη τῶν φύλλων συνείρουσι καὶ διαπλέκουσιν ἡδὺ μὲν ἐφήμερον δὲ καὶ ἄκαρπον ἔργον· αἱ δὲ πολλάκις ἴων καὶ ῥόδων καὶ ὑακίνθων διαπετόμεναι λειμῶνας ἐπὶ τὸν

player, but then gave him nothing on the ground that his promise had been fulfilled: "You were enjoying the hope of your reward for as long as I was enjoying your singing," he quipped.[18] The lectures I've been describing provide the same sort of reward to the speakers: They're admired for as long as they're pleasing to the audience; then, once the pleasantness of the lecture is gone, the speakers' glory vanishes too. And so, the audience has spent its time in vain, while the speakers have led pointless lives.

[14] We must, therefore, peel away the long-winded emptiness of style and seek the fruit itself, imitating not the people who braid wreaths but the honeybees. For the wreath-makers select the blooming and fragrant leaves of flowers and weave them into an artifact that, although pleasant, is also ephemeral and bears no fruit. The honeybees,

τραχύτατον καὶ δριμύτατον θύμον καταίρουσι καὶ τούτῳ προσκάθηνται "ξανθὸν μέλι μηδόμεναι," καὶ λαβοῦσαί τι τῶν χρησίμων ἀποπέτονται πρὸς τὸ οἰκεῖον ἔργον. οὕτως οὖν δεῖ τὸν φιλότεχνον καὶ καθαρὸν ἀκροατὴν τὰ μὲν ἀνθηρὰ καὶ τρυφερὰ τῶν ὀνομάτων καὶ τῶν πραγμάτων τὰ δραματικὰ καὶ πανηγυρικὰ κηφήνων βοτάνην σοφιστιώντων ἡγούμενον ἐᾶν, αὐτὸν δὲ τῇ προσοχῇ καταδυόμενον εἰς τὸν νοῦν τοῦ λόγου καὶ τὴν διάθεσιν τοῦ λέγοντος ἕλκειν ἀπ᾽ αὐτῆς τὸ χρήσιμον καὶ ὠφέλιμον, μεμνημένον ὡς οὐκ εἰς θέατρον οὐδ᾽ ᾠδεῖον ἀλλ᾽ εἰς σχολὴν καὶ διδασκαλεῖον ἀφῖκται, τῷ λόγῳ τὸν βίον ἐπανορθωσόμενος. ὅθεν δὴ καὶ ποιητέον ἐπίσκεψιν καὶ κρίσιν τῆς ἀκροάσεως ἐξ αὑτοῦ καὶ τῆς περὶ αὑτὸν διαθέσεως, ἀναλογιζόμενον εἴ τι τῶν παθῶν γέγονε μαλακώτερον, εἴ τι τῶν ἀνιαρῶν κουφότερον, εἰ θάρσος εἰ φρόνημα βέβαιον, εἰ πρὸς ἀρετὴν καὶ τὸ καλὸν ἐνθουσιασμός.

however, frequently bypass meadows filled with violets and roses and hyacinth, and they land instead on the spiky and pungent thyme. "Envisioning golden honey,"[19] they work the thyme diligently, and when they've extracted something useful, they fly back to the business of their hive. In just the same way, the authentic and devoted student must discount vocabulary that's flowery and extravagant and subjects that are ostentatious and dramatic, considering them to be fodder for drones who play intellectual games. The student must focus instead on the meaning of a lecture and the mind of the speaker, drawing from them what's useful and beneficial and being always mindful that they've come not to a theater or concert hall, but to a school and place of learning, with the aim of improving their lives through what's being taught. We ought, therefore, to judge

οὐ γὰρ ἐκ κουρείου μὲν ἀναστάντα δεῖ τῷ κατόπτρῳ παραστῆναι καὶ τῆς κεφαλῆς ἅψασθαι, τὴν περικοπὴν τῶν τριχῶν ἐπισκοποῦντα καὶ τῆς κουρᾶς τὴν διαφοράν, ἐκ δὲ ἀκροάσεως ἀπιόντα καὶ σχολῆς οὐκ εὐθὺς ἀφορᾶν χρὴ πρὸς ἑαυτόν, καταμανθάνοντα τὴν ψυχὴν εἴ τι τῶν ὀχληρῶν ἀποτεθειμένη καὶ περιττῶν ἐλαφροτέρα γέγονε καὶ ἡδίων. "οὔτε γὰρ βαλανείου," φησὶν ὁ Ἀρίστων, "οὔτε λόγου μὴ καθαίροντος ὄφελός ἐστιν."

[15] Ἡδέσθω μὲν οὖν ὑπὸ λόγων ὠφελούμενος ὁ νέος· οὐ δεῖ δὲ τὸ ἡδὺ τῆς ἀκροάσεως ποιεῖσθαι τέλος, οὐδ᾽ οἴεσθαι

a lecture based on how it affects us and our thinking: Have any of our emotions been calmed or any of our troubles made lighter? Has our courage or resolve been strengthened? Have we been inspired in the direction of virtue and goodness? When we finish with the barber, don't we feel the need to inspect our head in the mirror, to evaluate our haircut and see what difference the trimming has made? If we do that, shouldn't we also inspect ourselves as soon as we return from a lecture or class, to discover whether our soul has been relieved of some of its troubles and excesses, and if it has become lighter and more pleasant? As Ariston says, "Neither a bath nor a lecture does any good if it doesn't make you clean and pure."[20]

[15] Let young people enjoy lectures, so long as they're deriving benefit from them. But they shouldn't make enjoyment their

δεῖν ἐκ σχολῆς ἀπιέναι φιλοσόφου μινυρίζοντα καὶ γεγανωμένον, οὐδὲ ζητεῖν μυρίζεσθαι δεόμενον ἐμβροχῆς καὶ καταπλάσματος, ἀλλὰ χάριν ἔχειν, ἄν τις ὥσπερ καπνῷ σμῆνος λόγῳ δριμεῖ τὴν διάνοιαν ἀχλύος πολλῆς καὶ ἀμβλύτητος γέμουσαν ἐκκαθήρῃ. καὶ γὰρ εἰ τοῖς λέγουσι προσήκει μὴ παντάπασιν ἡδονὴν ἐχούσης καὶ πιθανότητα λέξεως παραμελεῖν, ἐλάχιστα τούτου φροντιστέον τῷ νέῳ, τό γε πρῶτον. ὕστερον δέ που, καθάπερ οἱ πίνοντες, ὅταν παύσωνται διψῶντες, τότε τὰ τορεύματα τῶν ἐκπωμάτων ὑποθεωροῦσι καὶ στρέφουσιν, οὕτως ἐμπλησθέντι δογμάτων καὶ ἀναπνεύσαντι δοτέον τὴν λέξιν εἴ τι κομψὸν ἔχει καὶ περιττὸν ἐπισκοπεῖν. ὁ δ' εὐθὺς ἐξ ἀρχῆς μὴ τοῖς πράγμασιν ἐμφυόμενος ἀλλὰ τὴν λέξιν Ἀττικὴν ἀξιῶν εἶναι καὶ ἰσχνὴν ὅμοιός ἐστι μὴ βουλομένῳ πιεῖν ἀντίδοτον, ἂν μὴ τὸ ἀγγεῖον ἐκ τῆς Ἀττικῆς κωλιάδος ᾖ

educational goal, nor should they think it necessary to leave a philosopher's class humming a tune or radiant with joy, just as they wouldn't expect to be anointed with cologne when they really need a healing ointment or a compress. Instead, they should experience joy if their mind, after being clouded with mist and dullness, is made clear by a penetrating lecture, just as we clear away a swarm of bees with smoke. For even if a speaker rightly adopts a style that includes some amount of pleasure and persuasion, young students should pay very little attention to that aspect of the lecture, at least when first starting out. Later, perhaps, they may act like people drinking from embossed vessels who, once they've satisfied their thirst, lift and turn their cups to observe their decoration. That is, after they've been inspired and filled with learning, then

κεκεραμευμένον, μηδ᾽ ἱμάτιον περιβαλέσθαι χειμῶνος, εἰ μὴ προβάτων Ἀττικῶν εἴη τὸ ἔριον, ἀλλ᾽ ὥσπερ ἐν τρίβωνι Λυσιακοῦ λόγου λεπτῷ καὶ ψιλῷ καθήμενος ἄπρακτος καὶ ἀκίνητος. ταῦτα γὰρ τὰ νοσήματα πολλὴν μὲν ἐρημίαν νοῦ καὶ φρενῶν ἀγαθῶν, πολλὴν δὲ τερθρείαν καὶ στωμυλίαν ἐν ταῖς σχολαῖς πεποίηκε, τῶν μειρακίων οὔτε βίον οὔτε πρᾶξιν οὔτε πολιτείαν φιλοσόφου παραφυλαττόντων ἀνδρός, ἀλλὰ λέξεις καὶ ῥήματα καὶ τὸ καλῶς ἀπαγγέλλειν ἐν ἐπαίνῳ τιθεμένων, τὸ δ᾽ ἀπαγγελλόμενον εἴτε χρήσιμον εἴτ᾽ ἄχρηστον εἴτ᾽ ἀναγκαῖον εἴτε κενόν ἐστι καὶ περιττὸν οὐκ ἐπισταμένων οὐδὲ βουλομένων ἐξετάζειν.

students may scrutinize a lecture's style, to see if it contains anything clever or extraordinary. However, the beginning student who's not concerned with the contents but demands that lectures be given in the plain, Attic style is just like someone who declines to drink medicine unless the cup is made from a special type of Attic clay, or who refuses to wear a coat in winter unless it's made from the wool of Attic sheep, and so sits unproductive and motionless, wrapped in a threadbare cloak as fine and delicate as a speech by Lysias.[21] This disease has created a great deficit of intellect and good sense, along with great pedantry and long-windedness in the schools, since young people take to heart neither the life nor deeds nor conduct of the philosopher. Instead, they're ready to praise style and expression and fine recitations, even though

[16] Ἀκολουθεῖ δὲ τούτοις τὸ περὶ τῶν προβλημάτων παράγγελμα. δεῖ γὰρ τὸν ἐπὶ δεῖπνον ἥκοντα τοῖς παρακειμένοις χρῆσθαι καὶ μηδὲν αἰτεῖν ἄλλο μηδ' ἐξελέγχειν· ὁ δ' ἐπὶ λόγων ἀφιγμένος ἑστίασιν, ἂν μὲν ἐπὶ ῥητοῖς, ἀκροάσθω σιωπῇ τοῦ λέγοντος (οἱ γὰρ εἰς ἄλλας ὑποθέσεις ἐξάγοντες καὶ παρεμβάλλοντες ἐρωτήματα καὶ προσδιαποροῦντες, οὐχ ἡδεῖς οὐδ' εὐσυνάλλακτοι πρὸς ἀκρόασιν ὄντες, ὠφελοῦνται μὲν οὐδέν, τὸν δὲ λέγοντα καὶ τὸν λόγον ὁμοῦ συνταράττουσιν)· ὅταν δὲ τοὺς ἀκούοντας ὁ λέγων ἐρωτᾶν καὶ προβάλλειν κελεύσῃ, χρήσιμόν τι δεῖ καὶ ἀναγκαῖον ἀεὶ προβάλλοντα φαίνεσθαι. ὁ μὲν γὰρ Ὀδυσσεὺς καταγελᾶται παρὰ τοῖς

they can't discern whether what's being recited is useful or useless, essential or vapid and superfluous, and they don't even want to find out.

[16] Let's turn to instructions for posing questions. When you're attending a dinner party, you must eat what's being served, without requesting something different or criticizing the food. And so, when you're attending a "banquet of words," you should listen to the speaker in silence, since that's why you came. Some people, however, like to draw a speaker off topic, pose extraneous questions, and raise other issues: They make for an unpleasant and disagreeable audience, since they derive no benefit for themselves, while they confuse the speaker and disrupt the lecturing. But when the speaker invites those in attendance to ask questions or pose their own problems, you must always

μνηστῆρσιν "αἰτίζων ἀκόλους, οὐκ ἄορας οὐδὲ λέβητας·" μεγαλοψυχίας γὰρ ἡγοῦνται σημεῖον, ὡς τὸ διδόναι τι τῶν μεγάλων, καὶ τὸ αἰτεῖν. μᾶλλον δ' ἄν τις ἀκροατοῦ καταγελάσειεν εἰς μικρὰ καὶ γλίσχρα προβλήματα τὸν διαλεγόμενον κινοῦντος, οἷα τερθρευόμενοί τινες τῶν νέων καὶ παρεπιδεικνύμενοι διαλεκτικὴν ἢ μαθηματικὴν ἕξιν εἰώθασι προβάλλειν περὶ τῆς τῶν ἀορίστων τομῆς, καὶ τίς ἡ κατὰ πλευρὰν ἢ κατὰ διάμετρον κίνησις. πρὸς οὓς ἔστιν εἰπεῖν τὸ ὑπὸ Φυλοτίμου πρὸς τὸν ἔμπυον καὶ φθισιῶντα ῥηθέν. ἐπεὶ γὰρ ἐλάλησεν αὐτῷ φαρμάκιον αἰτῶν πρὸς παρωνυχίαν, αἰσθόμενος ἀπὸ τῆς χρόας καὶ τῆς ἀναπνοῆς τὴν διάθεσιν "οὐκ ἔστι σοι," φησίν, "ὦ βέλτιστε, περὶ παρωνυχίας ὁ λόγος." οὐδὲ σοὶ τοίνυν, ὦ νεανία, περὶ τοιούτων ζητημάτων ὥρα σκοπεῖν, ἀλλὰ πῶς οἰήματος καὶ ἀλαζονείας ἐρώτων τε καὶ φλυαρίας

be seen as raising points that are useful and necessary. Odysseus, for example, was ridiculed by the suitors because "he was asking for scraps of food, rather than swords and cauldrons." The suitors believed that making a big request, just like granting one, was the mark of a magnanimous person.[22] There's even a better case for ridiculing students who compel a speaker to address issues that are trifling and trivial, like those hairsplitters who try to show off their skills in logic and math by asking questions about the division of infinite things or the motion of ambling and trotting.[23] To these types we may respond with what Phylotimus said to the man covered with sores and suffering from tuberculosis.[24] When the man asked him for a drug to treat his inflamed fingernail, Phylotimus diagnosed his condition from his complexion and his breath. "My good man,"

ἀπολυθεὶς εἰς βίον ἄτυφον καὶ ὑγιαίνοντα καταστήσεις σαυτόν.

[17] Εὖ μάλα δὲ χρὴ καὶ πρὸς τὴν τοῦ λέγοντος ἐμπειρίαν ἢ φυσικὴν δύναμιν ἡρμοσμένον, ἐν οἷς αὐτὸς ἑαυτοῦ κράτιστός ἐστι, ποιεῖσθαι τὰς ἐρωτήσεις, καὶ μὴ παραβιάζεσθαι τὸν μὲν ἠθικώτερον φιλοσοφοῦντα φυσικὰς ἐπάγοντα καὶ μαθηματικὰς ἀπορίας, τὸν δὲ τοῖς φυσικοῖς σεμνυνόμενον εἰς συνημμένων ἐπικρίσεις ἕλκοντα καὶ ψευδομένων λύσεις. ὡς γὰρ ὁ τῇ κλειδὶ τὰ ξύλα σχίζειν τῇ δ᾽ ἀξίνῃ τὴν θύραν ἀνοίγειν πειρώμενος οὐκ ἐκεῖνα δόξειεν ἂν ἐπηρεάζειν, ἀλλ᾽ αὑτὸν ἀποστερεῖν τῆς

he said, "an inflamed fingernail is the least of your problems." And so it is with you, my young friend: Now is not the time to be seeking answers to arcane questions. Rather, investigate how you may rid yourself of conceit and arrogance, break free of love affairs and other foolishness, and establish a way of life that's sensible and healthy.

[17] It's very important to consider your instructors' experience and natural abilities, and then to pose questions related to their areas of competence. You should not be forcing them out of their fields of expertise by, for example, asking a philosopher who's studied ethics to address problems in natural science and mathematics, or asking a natural scientist to give an opinion about the premise to a syllogism or solve the *Liar Paradox*.[25] If someone were attempting to cut wood with a key and open a door with an axe, we

ἑκατέρου χρείας καὶ δυνάμεως, οὕτως οἱ παρὰ τοῦ λέγοντος ὃ μὴ πέφυκε μηδ' ἤσκηκεν αἰτοῦντες, ὃ δ' ἔχει καὶ δίδωσι μὴ δρεπόμενοι μηδὲ λαμβάνοντες, οὐ τοῦτο βλάπτονται μόνον ἀλλὰ καὶ κακοήθειαν καὶ δυσμένειαν προσοφλισκάνουσι.

[18] Φυλακτέον δὲ καὶ τὸ πολλὰ καὶ πολλάκις αὐτὸν προβάλλειν· ἔστι γὰρ καὶ τοῦτο τρόπον τινὰ παρεπιδεικνυμένου. τὸ δ' ἑτέρου προτείνοντος ἀκροᾶσθαι μετ' εὐκολίας φιλόλογον καὶ κοινωνικόν, ἂν μή τι τῶν ἰδίων ἐνοχλῇ καὶ κατεπείγῃ πάθος ἐπισχέσεως δεόμενον ἢ νόσημα παρηγορίας. τάχα μὲν γὰρ οὐδ' "ἀμαθίην κρύπτειν ἄμεινον," ὥς φησιν Ἡράκλειτος, ἀλλ' εἰς μέσον τιθέναι καὶ θεραπεύειν. ἂν δ' ὀργή τις ἢ προσβολὴ δεισιδαιμονίας ἢ διαφορὰ πρὸς

wouldn't say that they're mistreating their tools, but rather that they're denying themselves the benefit of their tools' proper use and function. In the same way, students who don't appreciate or accept what a speaker has to offer and ask instead for things outside the speaker's competence not only harm themselves but also gain a reputation for mean-spiritedness and ill will.

[18] You must be careful not to pose too many questions, which is the habit of people interested in self-promotion. The scholarly and collegial habit is to listen agreeably while someone makes an argument, unless what you're hearing strikes a nerve, producing an emotional response that needs to be controlled or exposing a moral defect that should be treated. Perhaps in that case it's not "better to hide one's ignorance," as Heraclitus says, but rather to get your issue out

οἰκείους σύντονος ἢ περιμανὴς ἐξ ἔρωτος ἐπιθυμία “κινοῦσα χορδὰς τὰς ἀκινήτους φρενῶν” ἐπιταράξῃ τὴν διάνοιαν, οὐ φευκτέον εἰς ἑτέρους λόγους ἀποδιδράσκοντας τὸν ἔλεγχον, ἀλλὰ περὶ αὐτῶν τούτων ἀκουστέον ἐν ταῖς διατριβαῖς, καὶ μετὰ τὰς διατριβὰς ἰδίᾳ προσιόντας αὐτοὺς καὶ προσανακρίνοντας. ἀλλὰ μὴ τοὐναντίον, ὥσπερ οἱ πολλοὶ χαίρουσι τοῖς φιλοσόφοις περὶ ἄλλων διαλεγομένοις καὶ θαυμάζουσιν· ἂν δὲ τοὺς ἄλλους ἐάσας ὁ φιλόσοφος αὐτοῖς ἐκείνοις ἰδίᾳ παρρησιάζηται περὶ τῶν διαφερόντων καὶ ὑπομιμνήσκῃ, δυσχεραίνουσι καὶ περίεργον νομίζουσιν. ἐπιεικῶς γάρ, ὥσπερ τῶν τραγῳδῶν ἐν τοῖς θεάτροις, καὶ τῶν φιλοσόφων ἐν ταῖς σχολαῖς οἴονται δεῖν ἀκούειν, ἐν δὲ τοῖς ἔξω πράγμασιν οὐδὲν αὐτοὺς ἑαυτῶν διαφέρειν ἡγοῦνται, πρὸς μὲν τοὺς σοφιστὰς εἰκότως τοῦτο πεπονθότες (ἀναστάντες γὰρ ἀπὸ τοῦ θρόνου καὶ ἀποθέμενοι τὰ βιβλία καὶ τὰς εἰσαγωγὰς

into the open and address it.[26] Maybe you're feeling anger, suffering an attack of superstitious fear, having a sharp disagreement with a family member, or experiencing an intense sexual attraction "which pulls at even the most resistant heartstrings."[27] If something like this is disturbing your mind, you mustn't run off to a more comfortable lecture to avoid examining the problem.[28] Rather, you must attend lectures that address the very things that are bothering you, and even privately approach the speakers afterward to analyze your problems further. Don't do the opposite, which is what most people do: They listen happily and with admiration when a philosopher speaks about issues that trouble others, but then, when a lecture transitions to issues that hit close to home and deals with them bluntly, they become agitated and believe that the philosopher is

ἐν τοῖς ἀληθινοῖς τοῦ βίου μέρεσι μικροὶ καὶ ὑπὸ χεῖρα φαίνονται τοῖς πολλοῖς), πρὸς δὲ τοὺς ὄντως φιλοσόφους οὐ καλῶς, ἀγνοοῦντες ὅτι καὶ σπουδὴ καὶ παιδιὰ καὶ νεῦμα καὶ μειδίαμα καὶ σκυθρωπασμὸς αὐτῶν, μάλιστα δ᾽ ὁ πρὸς ἕκαστον ἰδίᾳ περαινόμενος λόγος ἔχει τινὰ καρπὸν ὠφέλιμον τοῖς ὑπομένειν καὶ προσέχειν ἐθισθεῖσι.

being meddlesome. This is perfectly reasonable, since most people think they ought to listen to philosophers while they're in school, just as they listen to actors while in the theater, but when it comes to nonacademic subjects, they believe that philosophers are no better than they are. This is a reasonable attitude with respect to sophists: Once they're out in the real world, outside the classroom and away from their books and prepared lessons, sophists seem to most people to be meek and insignificant.[29] But people who treat real philosophers this way are mistaken. They don't understand that a philosopher's seriousness and playfulness, the nods of approval, smiles, and scowls, and especially the instruction that's offered to each student individually, all provide a beneficial return for those who've learned to be patient and pay attention.

[19] Δεῖται δὲ καὶ τὸ περὶ τοὺς ἐπαίνους καθῆκον εὐλαβείας τινὸς καὶ μετριότητος διὰ τὸ μήτε τὴν ἔλλειψιν αὐτοῦ μήτε τὴν ὑπερβολὴν ἐλευθέριον εἶναι. βαρὺς μὲν γὰρ ἀκροατὴς καὶ φορτικὸς ὁ πρὸς πᾶν ἄτεγκτος καὶ ἀτενὴς τὸ λεγόμενον, οἰήματος ὑπούλου καὶ περιαυτολογίας ἐνδιαθέτου μεστός, ὡς ἔχων τι τῶν λεγομένων βέλτιον εἰπεῖν, μήτ᾽ ὀφρῦν κατασχηματίζων μήτε φωνὴν εὐγνώμονος μάρτυρα φιληκοΐας προϊέμενος, ἀλλὰ σιγῇ καὶ βαρύτητι καταπλάστῳ καὶ σχηματισμῷ θηρώμενος δόξαν εὐσταθοῦς καὶ βάθος ἔχοντος ἀνδρός, ὥσπερ χρημάτων τῶν ἐπαίνων ὅσον ἄλλῳ μεταδίδωσιν αὑτοῦ δοκῶν ἀφαιρεῖσθαι. πολλοὶ γάρ εἰσιν οἱ κακῶς καὶ παρὰ μέλος τὴν Πυθαγόρου φωνὴν ὑπολαμβάνοντες. ἐκεῖνος μὲν γὰρ ἐκ φιλοσοφίας ἔφησεν αὑτῷ περιγεγονέναι τὸ μηδὲν θαυμάζειν· οὗτοι δὲ τὸ μηδὲν ἐπαινεῖν μηδὲ τιμᾶν, ἐν τῷ καταφρονεῖν τὸ φρονεῖν

[19] Offering praise in the right proportion requires some discretion and moderation, since neither a deficiency nor an excess of praise is commendable. On the one extreme, there are the insufferable and onerous students who are stubbornly defiant in the face of every argument, filled with deep-seated conceit and predisposed to self-glorification, always thinking they could give a better lecture. They sit stone-faced and say nothing to indicate that they're receptive to what's being said, and with their affected silence, gravitas, and pretense, they try to earn a reputation for being unflappable and profound. They conceive of praise as though it were money: If they pay a compliment to someone else, they think it's been withdrawn from their own account. Many people, in fact, have misinterpreted the saying of Pythagoras and are out of harmony

τιθέμενοι καὶ τὸ σεμνὸν ὑπεροψίᾳ διώκοντες. ὁ γὰρ φιλόσοφος λόγος τὸ μὲν ἐξ ἀπορίας καὶ ἀγνοίας θαῦμα καὶ θάμβος ἐξαιρεῖ γνώσει καὶ ἱστορίᾳ τῆς περὶ ἕκαστον αἰτίας, τὸ δ᾽ εὔκολον καὶ μέτριον καὶ φιλάνθρωπον οὐκ ἀπόλλυσι. τοῖς γὰρ ἀληθινῶς καὶ βεβαίως ἀγαθοῖς τιμή τε καλλίστη τὸ τιμῆσαί τινα τῶν ἀξίων, καὶ κόσμος εὐπρεπέστατος τὸ ἐπικοσμῆσαι, περιουσίᾳ δόξης καὶ ἀφθονίᾳ γιγνόμενον. οἱ δὲ γλίσχροι περὶ τοὺς ἑτέρων ἐπαίνους ἔτι πένεσθαι καὶ πεινῆν ἐοίκασι τῶν ἰδίων.

with its meaning. For Pythagoras claimed that philosophy had taught him "to wonder at nothing," and the defiant students interpret this saying to mean that they should neither praise nor honor anyone.[30] And so, they think that they'll appear wise when they offer ridicule and respectable when they show contempt. Philosophical discourse, however, uses knowledge and research into the cause of every phenomenon to dispel the admiration and wonder that arise from bewilderment and ignorance, and it does so without sacrificing good humor, moderation, or human decency. Indeed, for people who truly and unwaveringly possess those good qualities, there's no higher honor than to show respect to someone who deserves it, no adornment more beautiful than to decorate someone else. People act this way when they've been generously acclaimed by

[20] Ὁ δ᾽ ἐναντίος αὖ πάλιν τούτων, μηδὲν ἐπικρίνων ἀλλὰ κατὰ ῥῆμα καὶ συλλαβὴν ἐφιστάμενος καὶ κεκραγώς, ἐλαφρός τις ὢν καὶ ὀρνεώδης, πολλάκις μὲν οὐδ᾽ αὐτοῖς ἀρέσκει τοῖς ἀγωνιζομένοις, ἀεὶ δὲ λυπεῖ τοὺς ἀκροωμένους, ἀνασοβῶν καὶ συνεξανιστὰς παρὰ γνώμην, οἷον ἑλκομένους βίᾳ δι᾽ αἰδῶ καὶ συνεπηχοῦντας. οὐδὲν δ᾽ ὠφεληθεὶς διὰ τὸ ταραχώδη καὶ πολυπτόητον αὐτῷ περὶ τοὺς ἐπαίνους γεγονέναι τὴν ἀκρόασιν ἀπέρχεται τῶν τριῶν ἓν φερόμενος· εἴρων γὰρ ἢ κόλαξ ἢ περὶ λόγους ἀπειρόκαλος ἔδοξεν εἶναι.

others; when people are stingy with their praise, they reveal just how impoverished they are and how much they hunger for praise themselves.

[20] At the other extreme are the students who form no judgment at all, but give their attention to individual words, even syllables, and shout their reactions. These flighty simpletons usually bring no joy to the speaker, but they always bring grief to their fellow students, who are roused to their feet contrary to their better judgment, compelled as though by force of shame to add their voices to the noisy response. In the end, these students derive no benefit from the lecture, since for them the occasion is confused and chaotic thanks to their uncritical praise, and they come away bearing one of three labels: In the context of the lecture hall, they're considered fakers, flatterers, or rubes.

[21] Δίκην μὲν οὖν δικάζοντα δεῖ μήτε πρὸς ἔχθραν τινὰ μήτε πρὸς χάριν ἀκούειν ἀλλ᾽ ἀπὸ γνώμης πρὸς τὸ δίκαιον· ἐν δὲ ταῖς φιλολόγοις ἀκροάσεσιν οὔτε νόμος οὐδεὶς οὔθ᾽ ὅρκος ἡμᾶς ἀπείργει μὴ μετ᾽ εὐνοίας ἀποδέχεσθαι τὸν διαλεγόμενον. ἀλλὰ καὶ τὸν Ἑρμῆν ταῖς Χάρισιν οἱ παλαιοὶ συγκαθίδρυσαν, ὡς μάλιστα τοῦ λόγου τὸ κεχαρισμένον καὶ προσφιλὲς ἀπαιτοῦντος. οὐδὲ γὰρ οἷόν τε παντελῶς οὕτως ἐκβόλιμον εἶναι τὸν λέγοντα καὶ διημαρτημένον, ὥστε μήτε νοῦν τινα παρασχεῖν ἄξιον ἐπαίνου μήτ᾽ ἀπομνημόνευσιν ἑτέρων μήτ᾽ αὐτὴν τὴν ὑπόθεσιν τοῦ λόγου καὶ προαίρεσιν, ἀλλὰ μηδὲ λέξιν ἢ διάθεσιν τῶν λεγομένων, "ὡς ἀν᾽ ἐχινόποδας καὶ ἀνὰ τρηχεῖαν ὄνωνιν / φύονται μαλακῶν ἄνθεα λευκοΐων." ὅπου γὰρ ἐμέτου τινὲς ἐγκώμια καὶ πυρετοῦ καὶ νὴ Δία χύτρας ἐπιδεικνύμενοι πιθανότητος οὐκ ἀμοιροῦσιν, ἦ που λόγος ὑπ᾽ ἀνδρὸς ἁμωσγέπως δοκοῦντος ἢ καλουμένου

[21] Judges presiding in court must hear cases without showing either hostility or favor. Rather, they must be intent on finding justice. In the case of philosophical lectures, however, there's no law or oath that prevents us from welcoming a speaker with kindness. Our ancestors even used to include Hermes among representations of the Graces, because they thought that listening to a speech above all required grace and goodwill.[31] It's just not possible for a speaker to be so completely ineffectual and off the mark that their speech doesn't contain something praiseworthy, such as an idea, or a summary of someone else's arguments, or the subject itself and the purpose of the speech, or the style and arrangement of the contents, "just as even the blooms of the tender gillyflower grow among the prickly broom-plant and the jagged restharrow."[32] Now, some people

φιλοσόφου περαινόμενος οὐκ ἂν ὅλως ἀναπνοήν τινα καὶ καιρὸν ἀκροαταῖς εὐμενέσι καὶ φιλανθρώποις παράσχοι πρὸς ἔπαινον; οἱ γοῦν ἐν ὥρᾳ πάντες, ὥς φησιν ὁ Πλάτων, ἁμηγέπη δάκνουσι τὸν ἐρωτικόν, καὶ λευκοὺς μὲν θεῶν παῖδας ἀνακαλῶν μέλανας δ᾽ ἀνδρικούς, καὶ τὸν γρυπὸν βασιλικὸν καὶ τὸν σιμὸν ἐπίχαριν τὸν δ᾽ ὠχρὸν μελίχρουν ὑποκοριζόμενος ἀσπάζεται καὶ ἀγαπᾷ· δεινὸς γάρ ἐστιν ὁ ἔρως ὥσπερ κιττὸς αὑτὸν ἐκ πάσης ἀναδῆσαι προφάσεως. πολὺ δὴ μᾶλλον ὁ φιλήκοος καὶ φιλόλογος ἀεί τινος αἰτίας εὑρετικὸς ἔσται, δι᾽ ἣν οὐκ ἀπὸ τρόπου τῶν λεγόντων ἕκαστον ἐπαινῶν φανεῖται. καὶ γὰρ ὁ Πλάτων τὸν Λυσίου λόγον οὔτε κατὰ τὴν εὕρεσιν ἐπαινῶν καὶ τῆς ἀταξίας αἰτιώμενος ὅμως αὐτοῦ τὴν ἀπαγγελίαν ἐπαινεῖ, καὶ ὅτι "τῶν ὀνομάτων σαφῶς καὶ στρογγύλως ἕκαστον ἀποτετόρνευται." μέμψαιτο δ᾽ ἄν τις Ἀρχιλόχου μὲν τὴν ὑπόθεσιν, Παρμενίδου δὲ

have delivered convincing encomia of vomiting or fever or even—by God!—a clay pot. If that's possible, shouldn't a lecture delivered by someone who's managed to earn the reputation, or even the title, of philosopher provide some inspiration or opportunity to an audience that's amenable and generously disposed to offering praise? As Plato says, every young person, one way or another, becomes attractive to the one who's fallen in love with them:[33] A pale youth becomes a "child of the gods," a darker one "manly"; an aquiline nose is called "royal" while a flat one is "charming"; and skin that's sallow is said to have an "olive complexion." Thus, lovers embrace and cherish their beloved, for love is like ivy in the way that it cleverly insinuates itself using any pretext. The serious student will always be even more resourceful in finding some reason for openly

τὴν στιχοποιίαν, Φωκυλίδου δὲ τὴν εὐτέλειαν, Εὐριπίδου δὲ τὴν λαλιάν, Σοφοκλέους δὲ τὴν ἀνωμαλίαν, ὥσπερ ἀμέλει καὶ τῶν ῥητόρων ἐστὶν ὁ μὲν οὐκ ἔχων ἦθος, ὁ δὲ πρὸς πάθος ἀργός, ὁ δ᾽ ἐνδεὴς χαρίτων· ἕκαστός γε μὴν ἐπαινεῖται κατὰ τὸ ἴδιον τῆς δυνάμεως, ᾧ κινεῖν καὶ ἄγειν πέφυκεν. ὥστε καὶ τοῖς ἀκούουσιν εὐπορίαν εἶναι καὶ ἀφθονίαν τοῦ φιλοφρονεῖσθαι τοὺς λέγοντας. ἐνίοις γὰρ ἐξαρκεῖ, κἂν μὴ διὰ φωνῆς ἐπιμαρτυρῶμεν, ὄμματος πραότητα καὶ γαλήνην προσώπου καὶ διάθεσιν εὐμενῆ καὶ ἄλυπον ἐμπαρασχεῖν.

offering meaningful praise. For even Plato, though unimpressed with the inventiveness of Lysias's speech and critical of its disorganization, nonetheless praised its diction, saying that "each of the phrases was clear and nicely turned."[34] You could also fault Archilochus for his themes, Parmenides for his verse-writing, Phocylides for his sparseness, Euripides for his long-windedness, and Sophocles for his unevenness, just as you could of course say of the orators that one fails to represent character, another struggles to provoke emotion, and yet another lacks charm.[35] Each of them, however, is praised for his individual strength and ability, by means of which they have all been able to stir and move their audiences. In short, students have ample opportunity to treat speakers kindly. And even if we don't vocalize our approval, many speakers are satisfied if we

[22] Ἐκεῖνα μὲν γὰρ ἤδη καὶ πρὸς τοὺς ὅλως ἀποτυγχάνοντας ὥσπερ ἐγκύκλια καὶ κοινὰ πάσης ἀκροάσεώς ἐστι, καθέδρα τέ τις ἄθρυπτος καὶ ἀκλινὴς ἐν ὀρθῷ σχήματι καὶ πρόσβλεψις αὐτῷ τῷ λέγοντι καὶ τάξις ἐνεργοῦ προσοχῆς, καὶ προσώπου κατάστασις καθαρὰ καὶ ἀνέμφαντος οὐχ ὕβρεως οὐδὲ δυσκολίας μόνον ἀλλὰ καὶ φροντίδων ἄλλων καὶ ἀσχολιῶν· ὡς ἐν ἔργῳ γε παντὶ τὸ μὲν καλὸν ἐκ πολλῶν οἷον ἀριθμῶν εἰς ἕνα καιρὸν ἡκόντων ὑπὸ συμμετρίας τινὸς καὶ ἁρμονίας ἐπιτελεῖται, τὸ δ᾽ αἰσχρὸν ἐξ ἑνὸς τοῦ τυχόντος ἐλλείποντος ἢ προσόντος ἀτόπως εὐθὺς ἑτοίμην ἔχει τὴν γένεσιν, ὥσπερ ἐπ᾽ αὐτῆς τῆς ἀκροάσεως οὐ μόνον βαρύτης ἐπισκυνίου καὶ ἀηδία προσώπου καὶ βλέμμα ῥεμβῶδες καὶ περίκλασις σώματος καὶ μηρῶν

merely present a friendly face, a serene expression, and an attitude that conveys goodwill and causes them no grief.

[22] This sort of behavior is now considered standard at every lecture, even when listening to speakers who are not up to the task. We sit still with an upright posture, our gaze fixed on the speaker and our body positioned for active listening; our expression is neutral, communicating neither arrogance nor discontent, nor hinting that we might have other cares or interests on our mind. In every work of art, beauty is fashioned when symmetry and harmony bring disparate elements together into a unified whole, while deformity is quick to appear when only a single element happens to be missing or out of place. So, when it comes to listening, it's not just the furrowed brow, the disgusted look, the distracted glance, the

ἐπάλλαξις ἀπρεπὴς ἀλλὰ καὶ νεῦμα καὶ ψιθυρισμὸς πρὸς ἕτερον καὶ μειδίαμα χάσμαι τε ὑπνώδεις καὶ κατήφειαι καὶ πᾶν εἴ τι τούτοις ἔοικεν ὑπεύθυνόν ἐστι καὶ δεῖται πολλῆς εὐλαβείας.

[23] Οἱ δὲ τοῦ μὲν λέγοντος οἴονταί τι ἔργον εἶναι, τοῦ δ᾽ ἀκούοντος οὐδέν, ἀλλ᾽ ἐκεῖνον μὲν ἀξιοῦσιν ἥκειν πεφροντικότα καὶ παρεσκευασμένον, αὐτοὶ δ᾽ ἄσκεπτοι καὶ ἀφρόντιδες τῶν καθηκόντων ἐμβαλόντες καθέζονται καθάπερ ἀτεχνῶς ἐπὶ δεῖπνον ἥκοντες, εὖ παθεῖν πονουμένων ἑτέρων. καίτοι καὶ συνδείπνου τι χαρίεντος ἔργον ἐστί, πολὺ δὲ μᾶλλον ἀκροατοῦ. κοινωνὸς γάρ ἐστι τοῦ λόγου καὶ συνεργὸς τοῦ λέγοντος, καὶ οὐ τὰ μὲν ἐκείνου πλημμελήματα πικρῶς ἐξετάζειν ὀφείλει κατὰ ῥῆμα καὶ πρᾶγμα προσάγων τὴν εὔθυναν, αὐτὸς δ᾽ ἀνευθύνως ἀσχημονεῖν καὶ πολλὰ σολοικίζειν περὶ τὴν

shifting body, or the impolite crossing of the legs that you must answer for and, therefore, be wary of, but there's also the nod, the whisper to your neighbor, the smile, the sleepy yawn, the bowed head, and every other similar gesture.

[23] When it comes to a lecture, some people believe all the work is done by the speaker and the students do nothing. A speaker arrives, so they think, fully prepared and having given great thought to the topic, while the students charge in and take their seats, oblivious and neglectful of their duties, as though they've merely arrived at dinner. However, it does in fact take some effort to be a courteous dinner companion, and even more is required of the good student. Indeed, the students are partners in a lecture and colleagues with the speaker. They ought not be meticulous in examining

ἀκρόασιν, ἀλλ᾽ ὥσπερ ἐν τῷ σφαιρίζειν τῷ βάλλοντι δεῖ συγκινούμενον εὐρύθμως φέρεσθαι τὸν δεχόμενον, οὕτως ἐπὶ τῶν λόγων ἔστι τις εὐρυθμία καὶ περὶ τὸν λέγοντα καὶ περὶ τὸν ἀκροώμενον, ἂν ἑκάτερος τὸ προσῆκον αὑτῷ φυλάττῃ.

[24] Δεῖ δὲ μηδὲ ταῖς φωναῖς τῶν ἐπαίνων ὡς ἔτυχε χρῆσθαι. καὶ γὰρ Ἐπίκουρος ἐπὶ τοῖς τῶν φίλων ἐπιστολίοις κροτοθορύβους γίγνεσθαι παρ᾽ αὐτῶν λέγων ἀηδής ἐστιν. οἱ δὲ τὰς ξένας φωνὰς τοῖς ἀκροατηρίοις νῦν ἐπεισάγοντες οὗτοι, καὶ "θείως" καὶ "θεοφορήτως" καὶ "ἀπροσίτως" ἐπιλέγοντες, ὡς οὐκέτι τοῦ "καλῶς" καὶ τοῦ "σοφῶς" καὶ τοῦ "ἀληθῶς" ἐξαρκοῦντος, οἷς οἱ περὶ Πλάτωνα καὶ Σωκράτη καὶ Ὑπερείδην

the speaker's faults, scrutinizing every word and action, while they themselves are unaccountable even as they misbehave and fail to be a good audience. Just as when playing ball, the person catching must coordinate movements with the person who's throwing, so at a lecture some coordination is also necessary, on the part of both the speaker and the students, if every participant is going to perform their duty.

[24] We must also be careful about how we express praise. For even Epicurus is disappointing when he reveals that letters from his friends would spark great applause.[36] And some are now introducing new phrases into our lecture halls, describing a speaker's delivery as "divine" and "inspired" and "unparalleled" on the ground that words like "fine" and "wise" and "truthful" are no longer adequate, even though these were the

ἐχρῶντο σημείοις τῶν ἐπαίνων, ὑπερασχημονοῦσι καὶ διαβάλλουσι τοὺς λέγοντας ὡς ὑπερηφάνων τινῶν καὶ περιττῶν δεομένους ἐπαίνων. σφόδρα δ᾽ ἀηδεῖς εἰσι καὶ οἱ μεθ᾽ ὅρκου τοῖς λέγουσιν ὥσπερ ἐν δικαστηρίῳ τὰς μαρτυρίας ἀποδιδόντες. οὐχ ἧττον δὲ τούτων οἱ περὶ τὰς ποιότητας ἀστοχοῦντες, ὅταν φιλοσόφῳ μὲν ἐπιφωνῶσι "δριμέως," γέροντι δ᾽ "εὐφυῶς" ἢ "ἀνθηρῶς," τὰς τῶν παιζόντων καὶ πανηγυριζόντων ἐν ταῖς σχολαστικαῖς μελέταις φωνὰς ἐπὶ τοὺς φιλοσόφους μετακομίζοντες καὶ λόγῳ σωφρονοῦντι προσφέροντες ἔπαινον ἑταιρικόν, ὥσπερ ἀθλητῇ κρίνων ἢ ῥόδων στέφανον, οὐ δάφνης οὐδὲ κοτίνου περιτιθέντες. Εὐριπίδης μὲν οὖν ὁ ποιητής, ὡς ὑπολέγοντος αὐτοῦ τοῖς χορευταῖς ᾠδήν τινα πεποιημένην ἐφ᾽ ἁρμονίας εἷς ἐγέλασεν, "εἰ μή τις ἧς ἀναίσθητος" εἶπε "καὶ ἀμαθής, οὐκ ἂν ἐγέλασας ἐμοῦ μιξολυδιστὶ ᾄδοντος." ἀνὴρ

markers of praise used by the likes of Plato, Socrates, and Hyperides.[37] This trend is repulsive, and it slanders the speakers by implying that they need aggrandizing and excessive praise. Even worse are those who swear an oath as though in a courtroom to bear witness to a speaker's performance. And no better are those who misinterpret a lecture's quality, when, for example, they call out to a philosopher "sharp!" or to an old man "genius!" or "fresh!" They're transferring to philosophers the compliments used for the playful and showy declamations from their school days, and they're paying superficial respect to sober-minded reasoning. This is like crowning a victorious athlete with a wreath made of lilies or roses instead of bay or olive leaves.[38] Once Euripides the tragedian was teaching a song to his chorus when one member

δ᾽ ἂν οἶμαι φιλόσοφος καὶ πολιτικὸς ἀκροατοῦ διακεχυμένου τρυφὴν ἐκκόψειεν εἰπών "σύ μοι δοκεῖς ἀνόητος εἶναι καὶ ἀνάγωγος· οὐ γὰρ ἂν ἐμοῦ διδάσκοντος ἢ νουθετοῦντος ἢ διαλεγομένου περὶ θεῶν ἢ πολιτείας ἢ ἀρχῆς ἐτερέτιζες καὶ προσωρχοῦ τοῖς λόγοις." ὅρα γὰρ ἀληθῶς οἷόν ἐστι φιλοσόφου λέγοντος ἀπορεῖν τοὺς ἔξωθεν ὑπὸ τῶν ἔνδον βοώντων καὶ ἀλαλαζόντων πότερον αὐλοῦντος ἢ κιθαρίζοντος ἢ ὀρχουμένου τινὸς ὁ ἔπαινός ἐστι.

[25] Καὶ μὴν τῶν γε νουθεσιῶν καὶ τῶν ἐπιπλήξεων οὔτ᾽ ἀναλγήτως οὔτ᾽ ἀνάνδρως

started laughing. "You wouldn't have laughed while I was singing somberly," he said, "if you weren't so insensitive and ignorant."[39] I think a civic-minded philosopher could put an end to an immature student's misbehavior by saying something like this: "You seem to me foolish and rude; otherwise, you wouldn't be twittering and dancing to the sound of my words while I'm trying to instruct you, advise you, or engage you in dialogue about the gods or the constitution or the government." Just stop and consider what it means that, when a philosopher is giving a lecture, someone outside the hall hears the shouting and cheering that's coming from within and wonders whether the praise is for an aulos player, a kithara player, or a dancer.

[25] You should not, however, accept reprimands and rebukes with indifference or

ἀκουστέον. οἱ γὰρ εὐκόλως καὶ ὀλιγώρως τὸ κακῶς ἀκούειν ὑπὸ τῶν φιλοσόφων φέροντες, ὥστε γελᾶν ἐλεγχόμενοι καὶ τοὺς ἐλέγχοντας ἐπαινεῖν, ὥσπερ οἱ παράσιτοι τοὺς τρέφοντας, ὅταν ὑπ᾽ αὐτῶν λοιδορῶνται, παντάπασιν ἰταμοὶ καὶ θρασεῖς ὄντες, οὐ καλὴν οὐδ᾽ ἀληθῆ διδόασιν ἀπόδειξιν ἀνδρείας τὴν ἀναισχυντίαν. σκῶμμα μὲν γὰρ ἀνύβριστον ἐν παιδιᾷ τινι μετ᾽ εὐτραπελίας ἀφειμένον ἐνεγκεῖν ἀλύπως καὶ ἱλαρῶς οὐκ ἀγεννὲς οὐδ᾽ ἀπαίδευτον ἀλλ᾽ ἐλευθέριον πάνυ καὶ Λακωνικόν ἐστιν· ἐπαφῆς δὲ καὶ νουθεσίας πρὸς ἐπανόρθωσιν ἤθους ὥσπερ φαρμάκῳ δάκνοντι λόγῳ χρωμένης ἐλέγχοντι μὴ συνεσταλμένον ἀκούειν μηδ᾽ ἱδρῶτος καὶ ἰλίγγου μεστόν, αἰσχύνῃ φλεγόμενον τὴν ψυχήν, ἀλλ᾽ ἄτρεπτον καὶ σεσηρότα καὶ κατειρωνευόμενον, ἀνελευθέρου τινὸς δεινῶς καὶ ἀπαθοῦς πρὸς τὸ αἰδεῖσθαι νέου διὰ συνήθειαν ἁμαρτημάτων καὶ συνέχειαν,

timidity. For some listeners take a philosopher's chastisement so carelessly and lightly that they laugh while being scolded and praise the one who's scolding them, just as freeloaders lose none of their eagerness and confidence even when their hosts are belittling them. Their shamelessness is certainly no proof of courage. Now, there's nothing dishonorable or unsophisticated in taking an innocent joke with grace and good humor when it's delivered playfully and in jest; in fact, that's very noble and judicious.[40] However, if someone can listen to a rebuke or reprimand meant to improve their character, administered with straight talk as though it were a bitter pill, and not be humbled, break out in a sweat, or feel dazed, and not sense a flicker of shame in their soul, but instead remain unmoved, flash a grin, or laugh it off, that's the sure sign of a young

ὥσπερ ἐν σκληρᾷ σαρκὶ καὶ τυλώδει τῇ ψυχῇ μώλωπα μὴ λαμβάνοντος.

[26] Τούτων δὲ τοιούτων ὄντων οἱ τὴν ἐναντίαν διάθεσιν ἔχοντες νέοι κἂν ἅπαξ ποτὲ ἀκούσωσι κακῶς, φεύγοντες ἀνεπιστρεπτὶ καὶ δραπετεύοντες ἐκ φιλοσοφίας, καλὴν ἀρχὴν πρὸς τὸ σωθῆναι τὸ αἰδεῖσθαι παρὰ τῆς φύσεως ἔχοντες, ἀπολλύουσι διὰ τρυφὴν καὶ μαλακίαν, οὐκ ἐγκαρτεροῦντες τοῖς ἐλέγχοις οὐδὲ τὰς ἐπανορθώσεις δεχόμενοι γεννικῶς, ἀλλ᾽ ἐπὶ τὰς προσηνεῖς καὶ ἁπαλὰς ἀποστρέφοντες ὁμιλίας τὰ ὦτα κολάκων τινῶν ἢ σοφιστῶν ἀνωφελεῖς καὶ ἀνονήτους ἡδείας δὲ φωνὰς καταδόντων. ὥσπερ οὖν ὁ μετὰ τὴν τομὴν φεύγων τὸν ἰατρὸν καὶ τὸν ἐπίδεσμον μὴ προσιέμενος τὸ μὲν ἀλγεινὸν

person who's especially servile and incapable of embarrassment on account of having had their bad behavior continuously reinforced. Criticism leaves no mark on their soul, which has developed a hard and calloused shell.

[26] There are other young people who have a disposition that's exactly the opposite of what I've just described. If they're chastised even once, they run away from philosophy, fleeing without ever looking back. They have the right basis for improving themselves, since they naturally feel shame, but they squander the opportunity through self-indulgence and soft living. They can't withstand criticism or accept correction graciously. Instead, they open their ears to the soft and gentle voices of flatterers and sophists, who charm them with pleasing words that offer no benefit whatsoever. This is like

ἀνεδέξατο, τὸ δ᾽ ὠφέλιμον οὐχ ὑπέμεινε τῆς θεραπείας, οὕτως ὁ τῷ χαράξαντι καὶ τρώσαντι λόγῳ τὴν ἀβελτερίαν ἀπουλῶσαι καὶ καταστῆσαι μὴ παρασχὼν ἀπῆλθε δηχθεὶς καὶ ἀλγήσας ἐκ φιλοσοφίας, ὠφεληθεὶς δὲ μηδέν. οὐ γὰρ μόνον, ὡς Εὐριπίδης φησί, τὸ Τηλέφου τραῦμα “πριστοῖσι λόγχης θέλγεται ῥινήμασιν,” ἀλλὰ καὶ τὸν ἐκ φιλοσοφίας ἐμφυόμενον εὐφυέσι νέοις δηγμὸν αὐτὸς ὁ τρώσας λόγος ἰᾶται. διὸ δεῖ πάσχειν μέν τι καὶ δάκνεσθαι, μὴ συντρίβεσθαι δὲ μηδ᾽ ἀθυμεῖν τὸν ἐλεγχόμενον, ἀλλ᾽ ὥσπερ ἐν τελετῇ κατηργμένης αὐτοῦ φιλοσοφίας τοὺς πρώτους καθαρμοὺς καὶ θορύβους ἀνασχόμενον ἐλπίζειν τι γλυκὺ καὶ λαμπρὸν ἐκ τῆς παρούσης ἀδημονίας καὶ ταραχῆς. καὶ γὰρ ἂν ἀδίκως ἡ ἐπιτίμησις γίγνεσθαι δοκῇ, καλὸν ἀνασχέσθαι καὶ διακαρτερῆσαι λέγοντος· παυσαμένῳ δ᾽ αὐτὸν ἐντυχεῖν ἀπολογούμενον καὶ δεόμενον τὴν παρρησίαν

walking away after a surgeon makes an incision and not accepting the bandage, feeling all the pain but being too impatient to experience the healing that comes with treatment. In the same way, when a student has some moral failing that's been cut open by a speaker's incisive criticism but doesn't allow that same criticism to help the wound scar over and heal, the student walks away from philosophy with a biting pain but absolutely no benefit. For as Euripides says, Telephus's wound "was healed by filings shaved from the spear."[41] In the same way, the biting pain imparted by philosophy into clever students is healed by the very words that caused the wound. And so, you must suffer and feel the bite of pain, but when you've been criticized, you must not be crushed or disheartened. Rather, as though philosophy were consecrating you in a

ἐκείνην καὶ τὸν τόνον, ᾧ νῦν κέχρηται πρὸς αὐτόν, εἴς τι τῶν ἀληθῶς ἁμαρτανομένων φυλάττειν.

[27] Ἔτι τοίνυν ὥσπερ ἐν γράμμασι καὶ περὶ λύραν καὶ παλαίστραν αἱ πρῶται μαθήσεις πολὺν ἔχουσι θόρυβον καὶ πόνον καὶ ἀσάφειαν, εἶτα προιόντι κατὰ μικρὸν ὥσπερ πρὸς ἀνθρώπους συνήθεια πολλὴ καὶ γνῶσις ἐγγενομένη πάντα φίλα καὶ χειροήθη καὶ ῥᾴδια λέγειν τε καὶ πράττειν παρέσχεν, οὕτω δὴ καὶ φιλοσοφίας ἐχούσης τι καὶ γλίσχρον

religious ritual, you must endure the bewilderment of the initial purification in the hope of experiencing the sweetness and joy that come from your distress and confusion. For even if a rebuke seems to you undeserved, it's best to persevere and continue listening. Then, when the lecture's over, you should approach the philosopher and defend yourself, and you should ask that the frank speech and serious tone, which have just been used against you, be saved for addressing your actual faults.

[27] Also consider this example: When learning to read, to play the lyre, or to wrestle, the early lessons involve much confusion and toil and uncertainty, but then as you make steady progress there develops a real familiarity and knowledge—as also happens when forming friendships—that makes everything about the activity agreeable,

ἀμέλει καὶ ἀσύνηθες ἐν τοῖς πρώτοις ὀνόμασι καὶ πράγμασιν οὐ δεῖ φοβηθέντα τὰς ἀρχὰς ψοφοδεῶς καὶ ἀτόλμως ἐγκαταλιπεῖν, ἀλλὰ πειρώμενον ἑκάστου καὶ προσλιπαροῦντα καὶ γλιχόμενον τοῦ πρόσω τὴν πᾶν τὸ καλὸν ἡδὺ ποιοῦσαν ἀναμένειν συνήθειαν. ἥξει γὰρ οὐ διὰ μακροῦ πολὺ φῶς ἐπιφέρουσα τῇ μαθήσει καὶ δεινοὺς ἔρωτας ἐνδιδοῦσα πρὸς τὴν ἀρετήν, ὧν ἄνευ πάνυ τλήμονος ἀνδρός ἐστιν ἢ δειλοῦ τὸν ἄλλον ὑπομένειν βίον, ἐκπεσόντα δι᾽ ἀνανδρίαν φιλοσοφίας.

[28] Ἴσως μὲν οὖν ἔχει τι καὶ τὰ πράγματα τοῖς ἀπείροις καὶ νέοις ἐν ἀρχῇ δυσκατανόητον· οὐ μὴν ἀλλὰ τῇ γε πλείστῃ περιπίπτουσιν

manageable, and easy to perform. So it is with philosophy, which of course includes basic terminology and subject matter that are tricky and unfamiliar, but you shouldn't timidly abandon those early lessons out of fear or cowardice. Rather, you should always give your best effort, and you should persevere and cling to your progress as you await the familiarity that makes everything that's worthwhile seem pleasant. For familiarity won't take long to arrive, and when it comes, it will illuminate your path to education and instill in you a fierce desire for virtue. Conversely, the wholly miserable or fainthearted people who lack this desire are destined to live the rest of their lives devoid of philosophy because of their cowardice.

[28] In the beginning, of course, lectures may well deal with subjects that are difficult for young and inexperienced students to

ἀσαφείᾳ καὶ ἀγνοίᾳ δι᾽ αὐτούς, ἀπ᾽ ἐναντίων φύσεων ταὐτὸν ἁμαρτάνοντες. οἱ μὲν γὰρ αἰσχύνῃ τινὶ καὶ φειδοῖ τοῦ λέγοντος ὀκνοῦντες ἀνερέσθαι καὶ βεβαιώσασθαι τὸν λόγον, ὡς ἔχοντες ἐν νῷ συνεπινεύουσιν, οἱ δ᾽ ὑπὸ φιλοτιμίας ἀώρου καὶ κενῆς πρὸς ἑτέρους ἁμίλλης ὀξύτητα καὶ δύναμιν εὐμαθείας ἐπιδεικνύμενοι, πρὶν ἢ λαβεῖν ἔχειν ὁμολογοῦντες, οὐ λαμβάνουσιν. εἶτα συμβαίνει τοῖς μὲν αἰδήμοσι καὶ σιωπηλοῖς ἐκείνοις, ὅταν ἀπέλθωσι, λυπεῖν αὑτοὺς καὶ ἀπορεῖσθαι, καὶ τέλος αὖθις ὑπ᾽ ἀνάγκης ἐλαυνομένους σὺν αἰσχύνῃ μείζονι τοῖς εἰποῦσιν ἐνοχλεῖν ἀναπυνθανομένους καὶ μεταθέοντας, τοῖς δὲ φιλοτίμοις καὶ θρασέσιν ἀεὶ περιστέλλειν καὶ ἀποκρύπτειν συνοικοῦσαν τὴν ἀμαθίαν.

grasp. Even so, students most often fall into uncertainty and ignorance through their own fault, creating this situation for themselves by a couple of different, and opposing, natural tendencies. Some students, feeling a sort of shame and wishing to spare the speaker's feelings, hesitate to ask questions or clarify what's being said, and so they nod along as though they understand. Others are driven by inappropriate ambition and vain competitiveness with their fellow students. In their eagerness to demonstrate their acuity and capacity to learn quickly, they admit to catching the speaker's meaning before they really do, and so in fact they never get it. Those who feel shame and remain silent in lecture find themselves feeling distressed and confused afterward, and so they're compelled by an even greater sense of

[29] Πᾶσαν οὖν ἀπωσάμενοι τὴν τοσαύτην βλακείαν καὶ ἀλαζονείαν καὶ πρὸς τὸ μαθεῖν ἰόντες καὶ περὶ τὸ λαβεῖν τῇ διανοίᾳ τὸ χρησίμως λεγόμενον ὄντες, ὑπομένωμεν τοὺς τῶν εὐφυῶν δοκούντων γέλωτας, ὥσπερ ὁ Κλεάνθης καὶ ὁ Ξενοκράτης βραδύτεροι δοκοῦντες εἶναι τῶν συσχολαστῶν οὐκ ἀπεδίδρασκον ἐκ τοῦ μανθάνειν οὐδ᾽ ἀπέκαμνον, ἀλλὰ φθάνοντες εἰς ἑαυτοὺς ἔπαιζον, ἀγγείοις τε βραχυστόμοις καὶ πινακίσι χαλκαῖς ἀπεικάζοντες, ὡς μόλις μὲν παραδεχόμενοι τοὺς λόγους, ἀσφαλῶς δὲ καὶ βεβαίως τηροῦντες. οὐ γὰρ μόνον, ὥς φησι Φωκυλίδης, "πόλλ᾽ ἀπατηθῆναι διζήμενον ἔμμεναι ἐσθλόν," ἀλλὰ καὶ

shame to bother their instructors, chasing them down and finally asking their questions. The ambitious and reckless, meanwhile, always cover up and conceal their personal lack of learning.

[29] Once we've set aside all this sort of foolishness and arrogance, and instead find ourselves making progress toward learning and becoming intellectually receptive to useful lectures, let's also commit to enduring the teasing that comes from students at the head of the class. That's what Cleanthes and Xenocrates did.[42] When they were noticeably slower to learn than their classmates, they didn't walk away or give up on learning. Instead, they got ahead of their classmates by poking fun at themselves. They compared themselves to narrow-necked jugs (which take time to fill) and to bronze tablets (which require effort to inscribe): They may have

γελασθῆναι δεῖ πολλὰ καὶ ἀδοξῆσαι, καὶ σκώμματα καὶ βωμολοχίας ἀναδεξάμενον ὤσασθαι παντὶ τῷ θυμῷ καὶ καταθλῆσαι τὴν ἀμαθίαν.

[30] Οὐ μὴν οὐδὲ τῆς πρὸς τοὐναντίον ἁμαρτίας ἀμελητέον, ἣν ἁμαρτάνουσιν οἱ μὲν ὑπὸ νωθείας, ἀηδεῖς καὶ κοπώδεις ὄντες· οὐ γὰρ ἐθέλουσι γενόμενοι καθ᾿ αὑτοὺς πράγματα ἔχειν, ἀλλὰ παρέχουσι τῷ λέγοντι, πολλάκις ἐκπυνθανόμενοι περὶ τῶν αὐτῶν, ὥσπερ ἀπτῆνες νεοσσοὶ κεχηνότες ἀεὶ πρὸς ἀλλότριον στόμα καὶ πᾶν ἕτοιμον ἤδη καὶ διαπεπονημένον ὑπ᾿ ἄλλων ἐκλαμβάνειν ἐθέλοντες. ἕτεροι δὲ προσοχῆς καὶ δριμύτητος ἐν οὐ δέοντι θηρώμενοι δόξαν ἀποκναίουσι

been slow to take in the meaning of a lecture, but once they'd gotten it, they had it for good. For it's not only necessary, as Phocylides says, "to be tripped up over and over when you're striving to better yourself," but even to be frequently mocked and belittled.[43] However, you must endure the joking and taunting, while at the same time fighting with all your might to expel your ignorance.

[30] We shouldn't neglect to mention the mistake that leads to the opposite situation, one that disagreeable and wearisome people make out of laziness. For these types aren't willing to work through philosophical problems on their own, but they always present them to their instructor, repeatedly inquiring about the same things. In this way they're like young birds still in the nest: They stretch open their beaks in the direction of another bird's mouth, wishing to receive

λαλιᾷ καὶ περιεργίᾳ τοὺς λέγοντας, ἀεί τι προσδιαποροῦντες τῶν οὐκ ἀναγκαίων καὶ ζητοῦντες ἀποδείξεις τῶν οὐ δεομένων· "οὕτως ὁδὸς βραχεῖα γίγνεται μακρά," ὥς φησι Σοφοκλῆς, οὐκ αὐτοῖς μόνον ἀλλὰ καὶ τοῖς ἄλλοις. ἀντιλαμβανόμενοι γὰρ ἑκάστοτε κεναῖς καὶ περιτταῖς ἐρωτήσεσι τοῦ διδάσκοντος, ὥσπερ ἐν συνοδίᾳ, τὸ ἐνδελεχὲς ἐμποδίζουσι τῆς μαθήσεως, ἐπιστάσεις καὶ διατριβὰς λαμβανούσης. οὗτοι μὲν οὖν κατὰ τὸν Ἱερώνυμον ὥσπερ οἱ δειλοὶ καὶ λίχνοι σκύλακες τὰ δέρματα δάκνοντες οἴκοι καὶ τὰ τίλματα τίλλοντες τῶν θηρίων αὐτῶν οὐχ ἅπτονται· τοὺς δ' ἀργοὺς ἐκείνους παρακαλῶμεν, ὅταν τὰ κεφάλαια τῇ νοήσει περιλάβωσιν, αὐτοὺς δι' αὐτῶν τὰ λοιπὰ συντιθέναι, καὶ τῇ μνήμῃ χειραγωγεῖν τὴν εὕρεσιν, καὶ τὸν ἀλλότριον λόγον οἷον ἀρχὴν καὶ σπέρμα λαβόντας ἐκτρέφειν καὶ αὔξειν. οὐ γὰρ ὡς ἀγγεῖον ὁ νοῦς ἀποπληρώσεως

their food made ready-to-eat by someone else's effort. And there are others who, in the hope of establishing an undeserved reputation for diligence and eagerness, wear down their instructors with their chattiness and idle curiosity, always raising questions about tangential topics and seeking demonstrative proof for things that don't need proving. "Thus, the short road becomes a long one," as Sophocles says,[44] and not only for the idle talkers but for everyone else, too. For these students always slow the teacher down with their inane and excessive questions, and—to continue the metaphor of traveling—they obstruct the steady progress of learning, which experiences stops and delays. According to Hieronymus,[45] these students are like curious but timid puppies who chew on hides and tear out the fur when they're in the house, but outdoors

ἀλλ᾽ ὑπεκκαύματος μόνον ὥσπερ ὕλη δεῖται, ὁρμὴν ἐμποιοῦντος εὑρετικὴν καὶ ὄρεξιν ἐπὶ τὴν ἀλήθειαν. ὥσπερ οὖν εἴ τις ἐκ γειτόνων πυρὸς δεόμενος, εἶτα πολὺ καὶ λαμπρὸν εὑρὼν αὐτοῦ καταμένοι διὰ τέλους θαλπόμενος, οὕτως εἴ τις ἥκων λόγου μεταλαβεῖν πρὸς ἄλλον οὐκ οἴεται δεῖν φῶς οἰκεῖον ἐξάπτειν καὶ νοῦν ἴδιον, ἀλλὰ χαίρων τῇ ἀκροάσει κάθηται θελγόμενος, οἷον ἔρευθος ἕλκει καὶ γάνωμα τὴν δόξαν ἀπὸ τῶν λόγων, τὸν δ᾽ ἐντὸς εὐρῶτα τῆς ψυχῆς καὶ ζόφον οὐκ ἐκτεθέρμαγκεν οὐδ᾽ ἐξέωκε διὰ φιλοσοφίας.

they won't go near a living animal. Returning to the lazy students, let me encourage them to grasp the main points of any topic while listening to a lecture, and then to work out the rest of the lesson for themselves, relying on their memory of the lecture to guide their discovery of meaning. They should treat a lecture as a starting point, or as a seed, which they may then nourish and grow on their own. For the mind isn't like a container that needs filling; it's like firewood that only needs a spark to ignite a motivation for discovery and an appetite for the truth. Imagine that the fire has died in the home of one of your neighbors, and after they find a big, bright fire in another house, they remain there getting warm, without going back home. So it is for people who approach others to hear a lecture but don't think it necessary to kindle the light

[31] Εἰ δεῖ τινος οὖν πρὸς ἀκρόασιν ἑτέρου παραγγέλματος, δεῖ καὶ τοῦ νῦν εἰρημένου μνημονεύοντας ἀσκεῖν ἅμα τῇ μαθήσει τὴν εὕρεσιν, ἵνα μὴ σοφιστικὴν ἕξιν μηδ᾽ ἱστορικὴν ἀλλ᾽ ἐνδιάθετον καὶ φιλόσοφον λαμβάνωμεν, ἀρχὴν τοῦ καλῶς βιῶναι τὸ καλῶς ἀκοῦσαι νομίζοντες.

of their own mind. They sit enchanted, enjoying what they hear, and though they may form an opinion after listening, as we appear flush and bright after sitting by a fire, they haven't really warmed the moldy darkness of their soul or expelled the gloom by means of philosophy.

[31] If we need any other principle of listening, it's this: We must bear in mind what I've written above and practice discovering knowledge for ourselves even as we participate in lectures. Our aim is to acquire a habit of learning that's not merely academic or bookish, but fundamental to our character and grounded in philosophy. We must recognize, therefore, that listening well is the foundation for living well.

NOTES

Introduction

1 Plato, *Apology of Socrates* 38a: ὁ δὲ ἀνεξέταστος βίος οὐ βιωτὸς ἀνθρώπῳ.

2 *How to Listen* 30.

3 Porphyry, *Life of Plotinus* 3, 13.

How to Listen

1 By "come of age," Plutarch means that Nicander has formally adopted the special garment that would have marked his transition from adolescence to manhood. The Greek literally reads, "you've put on the clothing of manhood." If Nicander was following the Roman custom, he would have put on the *toga virilis*, the toga that was ceremonially adopted by young men during their teenage years. This transition

would have occurred before Nicander began to attend lectures on philosophy.

2 Plutarch is referring to a story found in the famous *Histories* of Herodotus. At *Histories* 1.8, Herodotus tells of a queen in Lydia whose husband, King Candaules, believed her to be the most beautiful woman in the world. In his eagerness to demonstrate her beauty, he made his most trusted confidant, a man named Gyges, hide in the queen's bedroom to watch her undress. The queen discovered Gyges, however, and felt ashamed that a man other than her husband had seen her naked. She gave Gyges a choice: He could be killed for dishonoring her or he could kill Candaules and take the king's place. Gyges chose to spare his own life, gaining both the queen and the throne in the bargain.

3 Theophrastus was a Peripatetic philosopher who succeeded Aristotle as head of the Lyceum, the Peripatetic school of philosophy in Athens.

4 Xenocrates was a Platonic philosopher and head of the Academy in Athens.

5 Bias of Priene (a city in modern Turkey) was one of the Seven Sages, an informal collection of wise men who lived during the archaic, or preclassical, period of Greek history. Amasis, king of Egypt during the same period, was also known for his wisdom and had friendly relations with many Greeks; see Herodotus, *Histories* 2.172–182. Plutarch wrote *The Dinner of the Seven Sages*, in which he imagines all seven Greek wise men at a social gathering in Corinth. While dinner is in progress, according to Plutarch's story, Bias reads a letter from Amasis asking him to solve a riddle posed by the king of Ethiopia (146f). Bias solves the riddle with a clever response that delights the other guests and, it is assumed, will be pleasing to Amasis as well. In his story of the dinner, Plutarch also includes the anecdote about Amasis asking Bias to send him the best and worst parts of the sacrificial animal. In another essay, *On Talkativeness* (506c), Plutarch relates the same anecdote, although in that version Amasis sends his request to Pittacus of Mytilene, another of the Seven Sages.

6 Wind eggs are unfertilized eggs produced by various birds, such as chickens and geese. In his essays *History of Animals* (559b–560a) and *Generation of Animals* (750b), Aristotle describes how and why they are produced. One theory, which Plutarch seems to be referring to and Aristotle disputes, is that wind eggs, like fertilized eggs, are produced through copulation but remain unfertilized. The name comes from an ancient idea that animals could be impregnated with the aid of the wind, but Aristotle and Plutarch are using the term only to describe unfertilized eggs.

7 Plutarch is quoting a line of poetry by an unknown author, perhaps the philosopher Empedocles.

8 Epaminondas was a general and political leader for the city of Thebes. Known for his dedication to duty, he led the Thebans to their greatest military victories. Plutarch held Epaminondas in such high regard that he made him the subject of his first book of *Parallel Lives* (which

has been lost) and used him frequently as an example in his essays on good leadership.

9 Plutarch may be referring to either Aeschines the Socratic philosopher or Aeschines the politician and orator, both from Athens.

10 Xenophon of Athens was a soldier, philosopher, and prolific author. Plutarch refers here to the *Oeconomicus*, Xenophon's treatise on managing estates that features Socrates as narrator.

11 Plutarch frequently quotes this saying by Plato, though it does not appear in any of Plato's surviving works.

12 In his dialogue *Alcibiades I* (133a–b), Plato uses the fact that one's own eye is reflected in the eye of another person to introduce the idea of examining ourselves by observing others.

13 Lysias was a speechwriter who lived in Athens. In his dialogue *Phaedrus*, Plato has Socrates listen to one of Lysias's speeches and then, after offering criticism, write his own version.

14 In his collection *Spartan Sayings* (215b), Plutarch attributes this remark to King Agesipolis II. King Philip of Macedon besieged the city of Olynthus, captured it, and then razed it to the ground in 348 BC.

15 Heraclitus of Ephesus was a philosopher who flourished prior to the lifetime of Socrates. Thus, he and others of his era are known as pre-Socratic philosophers.

16 The aulos was an ancient wind instrument often compared to the oboe.

17 Melanthius and Diogenes wrote tragedies in Athens, but their works have been lost.

18 The kithara, which gives us the English word "guitar," was an ancient stringed instrument with a sound box. Both Dionysius I and his son Dionysius II were tyrants of Syracuse during the late fifth and early fourth centuries BC.

19 A fragment of a poem by Simonides.

20 Ariston of Chios was a Stoic philosopher.

21 Lysias the speechwriter (see above, n. 13) wrote in a style marked by simplicity of expression and the absence of rhetorical flourish. For later scholars of rhetoric, he came to exemplify the "plain" or "Attic" style, named for Attica, the territory where Athens is located. The "special type of Attic clay" mentioned here is from Colias, a region in Attica that produced clay highly desired by potters.

22 Plutarch is quoting from Homer, *Odyssey* 17.222. In the poem, when Odysseus first returns home to Ithaca after twenty years away, he enters his house disguised as a beggar. The suitors are young men who, under the assumption that Odysseus will never return, pressure his wife Penelope to remarry and to select one of them as her husband. While they await her decision, they hold raucous dinner parties in the house, and they abuse the disguised Odysseus as a wretched lowlife. The story was so well known to Plutarch's audience that he only had

to mention "Odysseus" and "the suitors" for his readers to understand the context.

23 Literally, "what is motion by side and crosswise." Motion "by side" refers to four-legged animals walking with the legs on each side moving in unison, a type of movement often called ambling. Motion "crosswise" refers to moving with opposite legs (left-front and right-back, for example) working together, as with horses when they're trotting. Aristotle surveys various types of motion in his treatise *History of Animals*, book 1.

24 Phylotimus was a physician from the island of Cos.

25 The analysis of syllogisms would fall to philosophers who studied logic. The *Liar Paradox*, also a logical problem, is based on a statement such as "Everything I say is a lie," which if true must also be false.

26 On Heraclitus, see above, n. 15.

27 Plutarch is quoting a line from a lost tragedy.

28 Plutarch is conceiving of these sorts of problems as issues of character and ethics, and so he believes they should be addressed through philosophical discourse and self-examination.

29 Sophists had a reputation for valuing philosophy as a means of making money through teaching and having little interest in living the philosophical life.

30 Pythagoras, a pre-Socratic philosopher and namesake of the Pythagorean theorem, had many teachings attributed to him by later generations, but many aspects of his life and career are obscure.

31 See, for example, the *Relief of the Graces*, now housed in the Acropolis Museum in Athens. This early fifth-century BC sculptural relief, which Plutarch may have seen, is believed to depict the three Graces dancing while Hermes plays music on the double aulos. Hermes, as the herald of the Olympian gods, could be a patron deity of reason and speech, and the Graces, although often associated with physical beauty, could also

foster intellectual skills and render a person's speech more persuasive. In his essay *Advice to the Bride and Groom* (138c–d), Plutarch says that these same "ancestors" invoked Hermes and the Graces along with Aphrodite to watch over a marriage, so that erotic desire (Aphrodite) would be tempered by reason (Hermes), and couples would get what they wanted from each other through persuasion (the Graces) rather than by quarreling.

32 Plutarch is quoting verses from an unknown poem. The "prickly broom-plant" is the *Genista acanthoclada*.

33 Plato, *Republic* 474d.

34 Plato, *Phaedrus* 234e; on the speech, see above, n. 13.

35 The authors used here as examples would have been well-known to Plutarch's readers. Archilochus and Phocylides were poets, Parmenides a philosopher, and Euripides and Sophocles tragedians.

36 Epicurus, the philosopher who founded the Epicurean school in Athens, would apparently

receive letters that included philosophical discussions and read them to his students.

37 Plato and Socrates are the famous Athenian philosophers. Hyperides, also an Athenian, was an influential orator and politician.

38 The prize for victory in the Pythian games, held at Delphi, was a crown made of bay leaves, while victors in the Olympic games received a crown of olive leaves.

39 Euripides literally says, "while I was singing in the Mixolydian mode." This mode was known to be sad and somber.

40 Plutarch here writes "laconic," which we usually take to mean speaking very little and no more than necessary. Here he uses it in the sense of choosing words carefully.

41 Plutarch is quoting a line from a lost tragedy. According to legend, Telephus was stabbed in the thigh by Achilles, and his wound would not heal until it was treated with filings from the same spear that had inflicted it.

42 Cleanthes was a Stoic philosopher and head of the Stoic school in Athens. Xenocrates

was a Platonist philosopher and head of the Platonic Academy, also in Athens. Using them as examples demonstrates that even students who learn slowly can go on to become masters of philosophy.

43 Phocylides is known only from wise sayings written in verse, such as the one quoted here, that have been attributed to him by others.

44 Sophocles, *Antigone*, line 232.

45 Plutarch is referring to Hieronymus of Rhodes, a Peripatetic, or Aristotelian, philosopher.

FURTHER READING

Beck, Mark (ed.). 2014. *A Companion to Plutarch*. Wiley-Blackwell.

Hillyard, Brian P. 1981. *Plutarch, De audiendo: A Text and Commentary*. Arno Press.

Plutarch. 1992. *Essays*. Translated by Robin Waterfield. Introduced and annotated by Ian Kidd. Penguin Books.

Plutarch. 1993. *Selected Essays and Dialogues*. Translated by Donald Russell. Oxford World's Classics. Oxford University Press.

Roskam, Geert. 2021. *Plutarch*. Greece & Rome: New Surveys in the Classics, no. 47. Cambridge University Press.

Titchener, Frances B. and Alexei V. Zadorojnyi (eds.). 2023. *The Cambridge Companion to Plutarch*. Cambridge University Press.

Van Hoof, Lieve. 2010. *Plutarch's Practical Ethics: The Social Dynamics of Philosophy*. Oxford University Press.

Watts, Edward J. 2006. *City and School in Late Antique Athens and Alexandria*. University of California Press.

Xenophontos, Sophia. 2016. *Ethical Education in Plutarch: Moralising Agents and Contexts*. De Gruyter.